Toronto Sketches 7

Toronto
Sketches

Mike Filey

THE DUNDURN GROUP
TORONTO · OXFORD

Copy-Editor: Andrea Pruss
Design: Jennifer Scott
Printer: University of Toronto Press

National Library of Canada Cataloguing in Publication Data

Filey, Mike, 1941-
    Toronto sketches 7: "the way we were" / Mike Filey.

"Columns from the Toronto Sunday Sun".
ISBN 1-55002-448-5

1. Toronto (Ont.) — History. I. Title.

FC3097.4.F5494 2003   971.3'541   C2003-901076-7   F1059.5.T6857 2003

1   2   3   4   5   07   06   05   04   03

THE CANADA COUNCIL | LE CONSEIL DES ARTS
FOR THE ARTS | DU CANADA
SINCE 1957 | DEPUIS 1957

Canada

ONTARIO ARTS COUNCIL
CONSEIL DES ARTS DE L'ONTARIO

We acknowledge the support of the **Canada Council for the Arts** and the **Ontario Arts Council** for our publishing program. We also acknowledge the financial support of the **Government of Canada** through the **Book Publishing Industry Development Program** and **The Association for the Export of Canadian Books**, and the **Government of Ontario** through the **Ontario Book Publishers Tax Credit** program, and the **Ontario Media Development Corporation's Ontario Book Initiative**.

Care has been taken to trace the ownership of copyright material used in this book. The author and the publisher welcome any information enabling them to rectify any references or credit in subsequent editions.

J. Kirk Howard, President

Printed and bound in Canada.⊕
Printed on recycled paper.
www.dundurn.com

Dundurn Press
8 Market Street
Suite 200
Toronto, Ontario, Canada
M5E 1M6

Dundurn Press
73 Lime Walk
Headington, Oxford,
England
OX3 7AD

Dundurn Press
2250 Military Road
Tonawanda NY
U.S.A. 14150

Table of Contents

Mike Filey's column "The Way We Were" has appeared in the *Toronto Sunday Sun* on a regular basis since 1975. Many of his earlier columns have been reproduced in volumes 1 through 6 of Dundurn Press's Toronto Sketches series. The columns in this book originally appeared in 1999 and 2000. Appended to each column is the date it first appeared as well as any relevant material that may have surfaced since that date.

Roundabout the Roundhouse

On almost any day during the spring, summer, and fall (and to a lesser extent in the winter), Toronto's waterfront is a place of intense hustle and bustle. In amongst all this activity, the ancient Canadian Pacific Railway roundhouse sits quietly on the edge of the city's new Roundhouse Park. It seems to be waiting for its chance to join in on the fun.

The roundhouse was built by the CPR in the late 1920s, replacing an earlier structure on the site that was erected in the later years of the nineteenth century. The new roundhouse had been prompted, in part, by the fact that Toronto would soon have a new Union Station, a massive project that had been talked about for years. Although the idea was first proposed in 1905 (with an opening scheduled for 1908), work on the new station didn't actually begin until the fall of 1914. Thirteen years later, on August 11, 1927, to be precise, the first passenger train departed the station, taking Edward, Prince of Wales, and his brother, Prince George, to Edward's ranch in Alberta. It would take another three years before the new station would be in full operation.

In total, a full quarter of a century had passed between the federal government ordering the railways to build a new Toronto railway station and the actual opening of the station to the general public. It was assumed that with that opening passenger traffic would increase

This view, taken exactly seventy years ago from the roof of the still incomplete Royal York Hotel, shows Canadian Pacific Railway's new roundhouse, which is also under construction. Note the old baseball stadium at Hanlan's Point on Toronto Island in the centre background and the new grain elevator that had recently been completed on land reclaimed from the bay. These two structures have been demolished.

Similar view, 1999.

Locomotive 5175 awaits servicing at the historic CPR roundhouse.

tremendously. Therefore, to better service the increased number of locomotives that would be needed to haul the numerous Toronto bound trains more efficiently, both the CPR and CNR decided to erect new state-of-the-art roundhouses. (The CNR's was located west of the CPR facility and was demolished to make way for SkyDome.) In addition to having thirty-two huge service bays, an integral part of the new CPR facility was a massive turntable on which the engine and tender that had recently arrived from the east could be turned after servicing. This action allowed the motive unit to exit into the service yard and couple up to an eastbound train, thereby eliminating the need to loop the train in the city's western suburbs. With the arrival of modern diesel engines (which require significantly less maintenance) and the subsequent move of the CPR's rambling servicing facilities to new yards northeast of the city, the old waterfront roundhouse and adjacent shops became redundant. After much negotiating, the city acquired ownership of the roundhouse and the adjacent property.

While this was going on, plans for the building's reuse were being voiced. Not surprisingly, given the impact the railways have had on the development of our country and on the City of Toronto in particular, the most frequent suggestion was to convert the massive, one-hundred-thousand-square-foot building into a major railway museum. Some even suggested that it become a fully operational museum complete with daily steam train excursions from the museum site up the Don Valley. While no one could argue that this latter idea would be the most desirable end use, the tremendously large amount of money necessary to implement such a dream just wasn't there. Now an idea has surfaced that may just be the ticket to pumping new life into the complex. Steam Whistle Brewing Company is looking for a place to build a new microbrewery/pub/retail outlet. The owners have proposed establishing such a facility in a portion of the roundhouse. And they've agreed that a percentage of business earnings would go to help fund a transportation museum that would be developed for the rest of the structure. I know the purists will flip over this idea. However, until some philanthropist comes along with very deep pockets, I think the Steam Whistle proposal should be explored further. Hopefully the new tenant will breathe life into an old building that needs all the help it can get.

June 20, 1999

* Steam Whistle began brewing operations in the CPR roundhouse in March 2000. As yet, no action has been taken on the museum proposal.

Toronto's Maritime Past
on Display at the Pier

Recently, one of the city's longest serving agencies, the Toronto Harbour Commission, was replaced with a new organization, the Toronto Port Authority. Created by an act of the federal government in 1911, one of the Harbour Commission's first responsibilities was to enlarge the central waterfront area by relocating the old harbour headwall eleven hundred feet further south into the bay. New land was then created by backfilling behind the new headwall with thousands of cubic yards of material dredged from the bottom of Toronto Bay plus thousands of tons of rip rap from the many construction sites around the city.

With the onset of the Great Depression a few years later, officials decided to erect several new structures along the new waterfront as make-work projects. One of these buildings was a new freight storage shed for the Tree Line Navigation Company. Over the ensuing years, this building was used for a variety of purposes, including, in recent years, a couple of restaurants operated by Walter Oster. Then, in the summer of 1998, the north end of the old structure was given a new lease on life when it became the new home of The Pier, a reincarnation of the Marine Museum of the Great Lakes that until recently had occupied the last remaining building of the historic Stanley Barracks located on the grounds of the Canadian National

Exhibition. The Pier has been equipped with interactive displays, a kids' discovery zone, a variety of ship models, a selection of operating ship whistles, and much more. Why not pay The Pier (245 Queen's Quay West) a visit this summer?

July 4, 1999

Work on the Tree Line Navigation Company's new freight shed on Queen's Quay West nears completion in the spring of 1930.

In July 1998, the old freight shed was reborn as The Pier, Toronto's waterfront museum.

Charles Colenutt, a longtime Toronto Island ferryboat captain, checks out The Pier's model of the Atlantic liner *Mauritania*.

* In 2001, City of Toronto officials, desperate to save money and with no regard for a place to tell the story of the city's fascinating maritime history, decided to close The Pier. At the time of the updating of this article (January 2003) the building formerly occupied by The Pier remains empty.

Sir John A. Preferred the Queen's

I'm told that this is the busiest weekend the city has seen this year, with just about every hotel full to the brim, not a room to be had anywhere. One of the busiest is the Royal York Hotel on Front Street West, which is celebrating its seventieth birthday this year, having opened to the public on June 11, 1929. And while the hotel may be seventy years old, the land on which it stands has been the site of a hostelry for nearly a century and a half.

The first was known as Sword's and opened in 1853 in what had been a row of four brick houses. Sword's became the Revere House in 1860. Another name change took place just two years later when Thomas Dick, a local steamboat captain, purchased the old building, remodelled it, and offered it to the public as the Queen's Hotel. Under Captain Dick's expert direction the Queen's soon became Toronto's most popular hotel. It's interesting to note that one of the Queen's most frequent visitors was a young lawyer/politician by the name of John A. Macdonald. He took up residence whenever the Dominion government met in the old parliament building, which was located on the north side of Front Street about where the CBC building is now located. There's some suggestion that Macdonald nurtured the idea of bringing the provinces of Upper and Lower Canada (now Ontario and Quebec), Nova Scotia, and New Brunswick together as the new Dominion of

In this photograph, an ancient horse-drawn streetcar operating on the Sherbourne route passes the Queen's Hotel. The view looks west along Front Street from Bay c.1880.

The same view with the Royal York Hotel in the background and a modern GO Transit bus on the Brampton route.

Canada in the hotel's famous Red Parlour. The Queen's had the distinction of having the first hot-air furnace and the first elevator of any hotel in the young country. The Queen's also featured running water in each room (another first) and had the city's first business telephone.

During the American Civil War, spies for both the Union and the Confederacy met freely in Toronto, where they could discuss their respective plans with impunity. Some say that the plot to assassinate President Lincoln was first discussed in the old Queen's Hotel. While that claim has yet to be substantiated, it is known for certain that a plan to burn down New York City in retaliation for the destruction of Atlanta by Union forces was concocted by Confederate sympathizers during a meeting at the Queen's. In 1927, following Canadian Pacific Railway's announcement that it intended to erect the country's largest hotel in Toronto, wrecking crews began clawing away at the grand old "Lady of Front Street." Within a few weeks she was no more.

July 11, 1999

Hotel Spadina Finds New Life As Backpackers' Hostel

Last week I wrote about Toronto's magnificent Royal York Hotel and its predecessor on the Front Street site, the legendary Queen's Hotel. As I described in that column, the old Queen's vanished in 1927 as work began on the new 1,200-room, $18-million Royal York. One of the old Queen's contemporaries still stands at the northwest corner of King Street West and Spadina Avenue. In 1873 it was known as the Richardson House and was operated by Samuel Richardson, described in the literature of the day as having eleven years of foreign military service with the 13th Hussars. That same promotional piece went on to state, rather awkwardly, that the hotel, "when necessary, could room nearly 100 guests." Richardson died in 1904, and a few years later the name of the business was changed, first to the Hotel Falconer and then to the Ziegler Hotel. Perhaps because the name was too German sounding, it was changed in 1917 to the Hotel Spadina, a name that was altered ever so slightly some years later to the Spadina Hotel. During the next eight decades, the hotel had a roller-coaster existence before a $250,000 renovation completed last year transformed it into a 200-bed youth hostel called Global Village Backpackers.

Just eight years after the hotel opened, the original Spadina streetcar line went into service. Streetcars continued to operate in the middle of this broad thoroughfare until replaced by buses in 1948. Their

A track crew is seen rebuilding the King-Spadina intersection in 1921. This was one of the first projects undertaken by the newly established TTC, which began operations on September 1, 1921. One of Toronto's oldest hostelries, identified in this photo as the Hotel Spadina, is seen in the background.

abandonment was an effort to conserve electricity, which was in short supply following the end of the Second World War. The electric streetcar returned to Spadina Avenue with great ceremony on July 27, 1997. The King streetcar route is even older than the one on Spadina, having been established in 1874. In fact, it was the third to be established (after Yonge and Queen) and initially ran from the Don River to Bathurst Street. It remains to this day as one of the TTC's busiest streetcar routes.

July 18, 1999

This view was taken shortly before the TTC decided to abandon the Spadina streetcar line in 1948 as an energy conservation measure.

The Hotel Spadina was recently transformed into a youth hostel known as Global Village Backpackers.

About the Man and Street Called Jarvis

Today, Jarvis Street is one of the busiest of the city's downtown thoroughfares. With that in mind, it's hard to believe that a little more than a century and a half ago, this same street was simply a narrow, dirt-covered pathway leading from Queen Street (then called Lot Street because of the large hundred-acre park lots that fronted on it) northward to the residence of one of the young city's most prominent families, which stood near the modern Jarvis and Shuter intersection.

The house, called Hazelburn, was erected in 1824 by Samuel Peters Jarvis, the son of William Jarvis, a prominent provincial government official who had been a member of John Graves Simcoe's Queen's Rangers and had fought against the Americans during the Revolutionary War. Following the end of hostilities, Jarvis returned to England. When his friend Simcoe was appointed governor of the new Province of Upper Canada, Jarvis was asked to assume a couple of plum appointments in the new provincial government. Accepting the offer, he crossed the Atlantic once more and took up residence in Newark (now Niagara-on-the-Lake), the capital of Simcoe's new province. Shortly after moving to Newark, William's wife, Hannah, gave birth to a son, Samuel Peters Jarvis, and in 1798 the Jarvis family moved across Lake Ontario to Simcoe's recently established Town of York. William actually undertook this move with great reluctance, since York was still a very primitive place, whereas Newark had evolved into a pleasant and quite fashionable place in which to live.

To ease the burden of having to relocate to the austere and uncomfortable town site across the lake, Simcoe gave his senior officials large

Jarvis Street looking north over King Street, c.1875. The building to the left of the photograph (with the words PURE TEAS COFFEE) is the St. Lawrence Hall. On the opposite corner the old building with the partial word PRINT-ERS painted on the wall has been restored and is now a retail store adjacent to the new King George Square condominium development.

The same view in 1999.

grants of land in and around York. Some revisionist historians have criticized the governor for this action. Others agree that this gesture was appropriate and necessary to ensure that the hierarchy was in place to guarantee the success of the little town's future. William Jarvis was initially given Lot 3 near the Don River, which he soon exchanged for Lot 6 some distance to the west. This latter property stretched north one and a quarter miles from Lot Street to the first concession road, a thoroughfare now called Bloor Street. Shortly before he died on August 13, 1817, William transferred his property to his son, Samuel, and the younger Jarvis built for himself a substantial two-storey brick house. Access to his new house was via a driveway off Lot Street. Soon after the house was demolished in 1847, that driveway was extended north to Bloor and given a name. Jarvis Street was born.

One other interesting fact about Samuel Peters Jarvis is that he holds the distinction of being the "winner" of Toronto's last duel. That incident occurred on July 12, 1817, out in the countryside north and west of the little town, a location not far from the present Bay and College Streets intersection. The victim was poor John Ridout, a member of another prominent local family, who, it is said, had in some way defamed the Jarvis family name. Following the duel, and as required by law, Jarvis was arrested for murder (a charge subsequently changed to manslaughter), jailed, and then tried by a jury of his peers. As it turned out, since all the formalities required for a duel to be considered "legal" had been properly followed, Samuel Jarvis was acquitted of all charges. The whole story of this fascinating Toronto family can be found in Austin Seton Thompson's marvellous book *Jarvis Street, A Story of Triumph and Tragedy*.

July 25, 1999

The Road Through Mount Pleasant

One of Toronto's pioneer cemeteries is the Necropolis, located at the east end of Winchester Street overlooking the Bayview Extension, the Don River, and the Don Valley Parkway. It was established in the early 1850s, and its owners, the trustees of the Toronto General Burying Grounds (now the Mount Pleasant Group of Cemeteries), were convinced that this location would provide sufficient accommodation for the departed for many years to come. How wrong their forecasts were.

Less than twenty-five years after the Necropolis opened, the trustees were on the hunt for new and larger facilities. And this time, to ensure they would not run out of burial space for as far as they could predict, the trustees decided to purchase, for the sum of $20,000, a 200-acre farm located well north of the city in the suburban community of Deer Park. Work on transforming the sprawling farm into a beautifully landscaped cemetery began in the spring of 1874. Pathways, driveways, bridges, and ponds were built, and finally, on November 4, 1876, the new Mount Pleasant Cemetery was formally opened to the public.

One thing the trustees had not counted on was the tremendous growth that would take place around their new cemetery — in particular, the rapid development of the north Yonge Street communities of Davisville, Eglinton, and Bedford Park that would soon join together and

City crews place streetcar tracks on the newly constructed bridge over the old Belt Line Railway tracks just north of Mount Pleasant Cemetery. Eight years later this bridge would become part of a new north-south thoroughfare called Mount Pleasant Road.

The same view, 1999. The tracks have been removed, the bridge replaced, and the future of the coal silos, built seventy years ago, is still unknown.

be known collectively as the Town of North Toronto. This growth soon prompted the locals to regard the cemetery — which ran from Yonge Street eastward one full concession (one and a quarter miles) to what was known as the First Concession East (later renamed the East York Road and later Bayview Avenue) — as a barrier that made their access to and from downtown Toronto more difficult than it needed to be. Residents began pleading with the township officials to have a road built through the cemetery. This request was, of course, contested by the cemetery trustees, who felt that such a project would diminish both the aesthetic quality of the manicured grounds and its monetary value. Arguments for and against a new road went on for years, and it wasn't until 1915 that an agreement was reached authorizing the construction of a quarter-mile-long, seventy-six-foot-wide right-of-way through the cemetery.

Two years later, a new dirt road that connected the existing dirt roads north and south of the cemetery was opened to both pedestrians and vehicles. A component of this new road was a new humped-back bridge over the Belt Line Railway tracks, which were now being used only by the occasional freight train. Anticipating that a new streetcar line would be eventually be opened on this thoroughfare, city work crews went ahead and laid tracks on the bridge. While they were at it, they also paved a small section of roadway over the bridge. This resulted in the Belt Line bridge being the only portion of the thoroughfare with an all-weather roadbed.

This situation existed until 1925, when TTC crews extended the existing streetcar tracks on St. Clair Avenue north on Mount Pleasant Road to a newly constructed loop at Eglinton Avenue. The city then proceeded to pave the rest of the roadway. The Mount Pleasant extension of the St. Clair streetcar route began on November 3, 1925. Streetcars were removed from the street in July 1976 and replaced by trolley buses that in turn were replaced by diesel buses. In 1928, three years after the streetcars began operating on Mount Pleasant Road, William H. Smith opened a new Dominion Coal outlet just north of the cemetery at the southwest corner of Mount Pleasant Road and Merton Street. One year later, the company erected the huge coal silos that have stood as industrial landmarks in the area for the past seven decades. Now known as Dominion Coal-Building Supplies, this long-time member of the north Toronto community will soon close. Then it will be up to the new owners of the property to determine the future of these unique silos.

August 1, 1999

* The silos were demolished in 2002.

Keeps on Track with a Unique Gauge

Every once in a while, somebody will ask me when and how my interest in Toronto's history began. Actually, I think it all started when I was a kid living on Bathurst Street not far from the busy Bloor Street corner. (Funny, I sometimes forget what happened two weeks ago, but I still remember my street address and even my phone number of a half-century ago: 758 Bathurst Street and MElrose 2154.) From the bay window of the family's third-floor apartment I could watch the streetcars trundle to and fro on the Bathurst route as well as check out the crosstown traffic on the Bloor-Danforth line in view just up the street.

Interestingly, while the Bathurst route is still operating and is now identified simply as 511, the Bloor-Danforth streetcars vanished with the opening of the Bloor-Danforth subway in 1966. It was from my vantage point three floors above street level that I could keep track of TTC operations, at least on these two streetcar lines. From this early start I developed an interest not just in the Commission's vehicles (though I did get know the difference between a TRC car, a Witt, and a PCC before I could pronounce the name of Stitsky's, the store next door to us) but also in just how the city grew as a result of the TTC's expansion of its streetcar and radial lines out into the suburbs.

It wasn't long before my interest in the city's transportation history grew into a less focused fascination with a variety of subjects dealing

In 1902, a delivery wagon driver for tobacconist Andrew Wilson manoeuvres his rig at Yonge and King Streets, keeping the wagon wheels in the streetcar tracks for a smoother ride.

with various aspects of Toronto's fascinating past. Then, thanks to all the excitement generated in 1967, the country's Centennial Year, my interest was given an extra boost and I began collecting old books on Toronto and seeking out ancient photographs and old postcards that featured city scenes from yesteryear. Just three years later, my first book, *A Toronto Album*, was published by U of T Press. It went through several reprints, ultimately selling several thousand copies, an indication that other Torontonians, long-time residents and newcomers alike, were also interested in their city's past.

But let's get back to the streetcars. While Toronto is recognized worldwide for several things (the birthplace of Mary Pickford, the world's first motion picture star, the site of the tallest free-standing structure on earth, and the home of the University of Toronto, where Doctors Banting and Best, and others, developed insulin), were you aware that our city has a unique transportation distinction as well? That distinction concerns the gauge (the distance between the rails) of the TTC's streetcar and subway tracks. While most of the world operates on a standard railway gauge, 4 feet, 8 1/2 inches, Toronto's streetcars and subway trains run on a slightly different gauge. And the old photo reveals why. Before the privately

TTC operator Frank Hood and friend check out
the gauge on which his historic PCC is operating.

owned Toronto Street Railway Co. began laying its first rails on Yonge Street in 1861, officials agreed that the distance between each rail would correspond to the distance between the wheels on opposite sides of the horse-drawn buggies and wagons then operating on the city's many streets. Since most of these vehicles were either English-built or built to English specifications and incorporated a 4-foot-10 7/8-inch (which was the standard in England) gauge, this automatically meant that the street railway gauge in Toronto would also be 4 feet, 10 7/8 inches. By adopting this figure the wagons could operate with both sets of wheels in the rail flangeways, rather than one set in the flangeway with the other set either inside or outside the other flangeway, where they would pound the pavement to pieces.

You can see in the 1902 photo that the driver of a delivery wagon owned by wholesale tobacconist Andrew Wilson (whose warehouse was at 43 Yonge Street) is following this procedure, and in addition to getting a smoother ride he is also helping to keep the brick-paved Yonge Street in relatively good repair. Interestingly, even today's modern subway lines operate using this same historic 4-foot 10 7/8-inch gauge.

August 15, 1999

An Exhibition with Tradition

Off and running for the 121st time is Toronto's own Canadian National Exhibition. Though first held in the fall of 1879 (it was then known as the Toronto Industrial Exhibition), the origins of our "Ex" actually go back to the year 1792. It was in the fall of that year that the first lieutenant-governor of the newly created Province of Upper Canada, John Graves Simcoe, began offering financial rewards to members of the Niagara Agricultural Society in an attempt to "encourage and improve" agriculture in the young province. One of our province's pioneer crops, and one that was deemed of particular importance, was hemp, which was used in the manufacture of rope, great quantities of which were required to rig the hundreds of sailing ships in the powerful Royal Navy.

The CNE has come a long way since then. This year the fair's main theme will be a salute to aviation, with displays and hands-on attractions in the exciting Flight Centre located in the Automotive Building. This year is also the fiftieth anniversary of the Canadian International Air Show, and during the last three days of the fair a special edition of what has become a major event during the annual fair has been scheduled.

While the air show is now a component of the CNE, that wasn't always the case. Before joining up with the Exhibition, shows were fre-

Considered modern in its day, the RCAF's de Havilland Vampire thrilled crowds at the very first Canadian International Air Show that was held fifty years ago this year.

quently held in the summer or early fall at Downsview Airport or across the city's waterfront. Then, beginning in 1956, the Canadian International Air Show became part of the annual Exhibition.

In that first year as part of the CNE's many attractions, the Royal Canadian Air Force's newest equipment, such as the CF-100 and F-86 Sabre jet fighters and the T-33 Silver Star jet trainers, was featured along with an assortment of older aircraft: Mustangs, Harvards, North Stars, Dakotas, and C-119 Packets. In addition, the Royal Canadian Navy presented a few of its new Banshee carrier-based jets. And although the French Magister jet trainer made it to the show, the Royal Air Force's

On June 27, 1977, the CNE's new flagpole was taken out of the Horticultural Building and positioned in place in time for that year's Exhibition.

sleek Hawker Hunters were no-shows due to the ongoing Suez Canal crisis. And with an attack over the North Pole by the mighty Russian air force still very much a possibility, the United States Air Force sent along a couple of their atomic attack "retaliation" bombers, the six-piston, four-jet engine Convair B-36 and the six-jet Boeing B-47, just to show they were ready. Visitors to the fair also got to witness in-flight refuelling for the first time when one of the B-47s coupled up to a KC-97 Stratotanker for a drink. The highlight of the show was a spectacular performance by the Navy's Blue Angels flying F9F Cougars. This team has returned many times to thrill Air Show crowds.

When I joined the staff of the CNE in 1974 as Special Projects Manager, one of my first assignments was to find a replacement for the CNE's wooden flagpole, which had been erected in 1930 and was now so full of dry rot that it was in danger of snapping in a stiff breeze. In late 1976, a giant 350-year-old Douglas fir that had toppled during a violent wind storm was discovered in a forest on Vancouver Island. Its massive root ball had prevented it from crashing to the earth and being smashed to pieces. There it lay in one piece. Thanks to Travel South, an organization made up of eleven southern states who had been exhibiting at the CNE for many years, we arranged to purchase the tree and have it shipped to the grounds. When the tree arrived at the CNE rail siding it was gently manouevred into the Horticultural Building, where, over the next few months, it was shaped into a 184-foot-tall flagpole. On June 27, 1977, the new wooden pole was positioned in the same huge stanchions that had supported the original flagpole for forty-seven years. The CNE's new main flagpole, flying the country's largest flag, was officially dedicated by Lieutenant-Governor Pauline McGibbon on August 18, 1977.

August 22, 1999

Major League Dreams of Yesteryear

Carlos Delgado, Shawn Green, and Darrin Fletcher; Jack Thoney, Ed Stevens, and Dale Alexander. All great Toronto major league baseball players. The first three are modern-day Blue Jays, of course, while the second three were members of the various Toronto Maple Leaf teams that, as members of the Triple A International League, played home games at the Hanlan's Point and Lake Shore and Bathurst Street stadiums of yesteryear. And then there was good old "Cannonball" Crane. "Cannonball" who? More about this amazing, but virtually unknown, ball player in a minute.

Nearly a century before anyone thought of playing under a roof (let alone one that moved) or on grass that wasn't, Torontonians were enjoying professional baseball at the city's first true baseball field. Known officially as the Toronto Baseball Grounds, this popular place was located behind a bunch of stores on the south side of Queen Street East, just steps west of the Broadview House hotel and the busy Broadview Avenue corner. This pioneer baseball field was laid out in 1886 and, to prove that baseball was a popular spectator sport long before either the Jays or Leaf teams began throwing a baseball around, came complete with a wooden grandstand in which 2,550 fans, each of whom had forked over an admission fee of 25 cents (plus another dime to sit in the centre reserved section), sat on cushioned seats and cheered the hometown boys to victory over teams from Rochester, Syracuse, Buffalo, and Hamilton.

The home opener at the Toronto Baseball Grounds (known first as "the park over the Don" and later, after the Lever company opened its soap factory south of the ball field, as "Sunlight Park") took place on May 22, 1886. The Toronto team, which had played the first few games that season at the old lacrosse grounds at Jarvis and Wellesley Streets, defeated the Rochester Hop Bitters (as close as you could get to promoting beer

This sketch (prepared c.1887) shows the Toronto Baseball Grounds in relation to streets and structures in and around the corner of Queen and Broadview. This rare view is from the collection of Canadian baseball history expert Dr. Bruce Meyer.

without stepping over the line, I guess) by a score of 10–3. Toronto pitcher "Peekaboo" Veach struck out five, belted a triple, and crossed home plate three times while allowing just three hits.

The Toronto Baseball Grounds remained home to the city's professional team until a new park opened at Hanlan's Point on the Island in 1897. Once the professionals left for the new Island stadium the historic field "over the Don" continued to be used for years by many of the city's amateur teams. One of the approaches to the park was via a small street running south off Queen that bore the exalted title Baseball Place. Recently, as the site was being redeveloped, the street (in reality, a laneway), the sign, and a nice collection of workers' cottages disappeared. Today, a car dealership occupies the former ball field. And while nothing remains today but memories, that'll soon remedied, when on Friday, September 17, Mayor Mel Lastman and Blue Jays President Gord Ash unveil one of Heritage Toronto's commemorative plaques honouring the Toronto Baseball Grounds, its players, and its fans.

Oh, I almost forgot the remarkable story of "Cannonball" Crane. This amazing athlete helped Toronto capture the 1887 baseball championship, the city's first, by winning both games of a Saturday double header (15–5 and 5–4). In the second game, Crane drove in three of Toronto's runs and, though injured, also hit the game-winning home run. Then "Cannonball" returned to pitch the following day's game, which the local boys won 22–8, thereby capturing the 1887 pennant. Interestingly, "Cannonball" Crane still holds a pair of professional baseball records, the first being the most wins in a season by a Toronto pitcher (33), the second for the highest batting average for a pitcher (.433). Later in life things started to go badly for the thirty-four-year-old, and in 1896 he decided to end it all by committing suicide.

Incidentally, you can learn lots more about Canada's part in the history of baseball by visiting the Canadian Baseball Hall of Fame and Museum in Street Mary's, Ontario. It's located in a century-old stone house, and artifacts, Hall inductees, and memorabilia highlighting our country's baseball roots are all on display. Call (toll free) 1-877-250-2255 for hours of operation or visit the Hall's Website at www.baseballhoffame.ca.

August 29, 1999

A Marine Disaster of
Titanic Proportions

As Torontonians awoke that Saturday morning of September 17, 1949, most were totally unaware that their city had just suffered through its worst disaster ever. The burning of the popular Canada Steamship Lines passenger vessel *Noronic* at its berth near the foot of Yonge Street in the early hours of the morning, and the appalling loss of life that resulted, would haunt the city for years.

The sleek *Noronic* had been built in the spring of 1913 at the Western Dry Dock and Shipbuilding yard in Port Arthur (now part of Thunder Bay), Ontario. With an overall length of 117.3 metres (385 feet), she was the largest vessel of her type to ever ply the waters of the Great Lakes. The vessel's unusual name was selected using the "No" from the name of its original owner, the Northern Navigation Company and "ro" from the "Richelieu and Ontario" component of the newly created Canada Steamship Line (that acquired the Northern in 1913). The "nic" suffix was common to the Northern Navigation Company's other passenger ships (*Saronic*, *Harmonic*, and *Huronic*). *Noronic*, affectionately referred to as the "Queen of the Lakes" by her many repeat patrons, usually operated on the Detroit–Sarnia–Duluth–Port Arthur route, with her visits to the Port of Toronto few and far between. In fact, the first didn't occur until June 10, 1931.

Noronic was a magnificent sight during her first visit to Toronto in June 1931.

Noronic would return in September 1949 for an overnight stay during what had been advertised as a leisurely cruise from the American cities of Detroit and Cleveland to Prescott and the beautiful Thousand Islands. *Noronic* arrived early in the evening of September 16, glided into Toronto Harbour, and made for Pier 9, where she tied up for the night. Many of her passengers decided to go ashore for some sightseeing and a sampling of the city's nightlife. By midnight, most had returned. Now it was quiet. At about 1:15 A.M., smoke was seen drifting out from under the door of a linen closet on C deck. The door was opened, searing flames erupted, and within minutes the stern of the vessel was turned into what was for many their funeral pyre. Confusion reigned. No telephone land line was in place, and it wasn't until a passerby on shore rang in the alarm that city firefighters were made aware of the unfolding disaster. Once notified, however, they were on the scene in minutes. But it was too late. The ship was totally engulfed in flames. The dozens of coats of paint and varnish applied to her beautiful wood panels and trimmings during the aging vessel's thirty-six-year history had sealed her fate.

When the flames were finally extinguished hours later, 118 passengers, all Americans, were dead. Dozens more were in agony. (The

Even before the Toronto Fire Department arrived on the scene, the Great Lakes' passenger vessel *Noronic* was totally engulfed in flames.

death toll rose by one several days later when a female member of the crew died as a result of her burns. Out of a crew complement of 171, she was the only fatality and the only Canadian lost in the tragedy.) The intensity of the flames resulted many of the victims being so badly burned that identification was impossible. Their remains were placed in a mass grave in Toronto's Mount Pleasant Cemetery.

September 5, 1999

*In the fall of 1999, an Ontario Heritage Foundation plaque was unveiled by three of the ship's survivors not far from the site of the *Noronic* disaster that had shocked two nations a half-century before.

100 Years and Counting:
Ceremonies to Mark Centennial
of Magnificent Old City Hall

I t was September 18, 1899, and Toronto Mayor John Shaw had had just about enough. Work on the city's new municipal building had been dragging on for years. Now, though it wasn't completely ready for occupation, the Chief Magistrate had decided it was time to move from the antiquated old City Hall at Front and Jarvis streets to the magnificent new City Hall–Court House complex at the top of Bay Street. Accompanied by two dozen or so council members and civic officials, the white-whiskered Shaw boarded one of two waiting horse-drawn streetcars outside his office and, along with the rest of the entourage, made his way uptown to the new building. Then, as the event was described in the *Evening Telegram* newspaper of the day, "with a handsome, chaste gold key of large proportions Mayor Shaw metaphorically unlocked the big door at the main entrance of the new municipal buildings at three o'clock this afternoon. As the massive oak door swung wide, his Worship formally declared the buildings open for the public transaction of the business of the municipality for all times."

Actually, Mayor Shaw was a bit too optimistic with the last part of the statement since another new City Hall would open for business sixty-six years later. Nevertheless, just how Toronto's Old City Hall came to be is a long, tangled, and, yes, interesting story. In the decade between 1874 and 1884 Toronto's population had grown from 68,000

The four gargoyles on the clock tower, which were removed some seventy years ago, have recently been replaced.

Court House/City Hall architect Edward James Lennox.

to 105,000. As a result of this rapid growth, it had become painfully obvious that the old municipal buildings at the southwest corner of Front and Jarvis streets, in use since the mid-1840s, had become obsolete. So, too, was the old York County Court House on Adelaide Street East. In fact, the courthouse was in such an unsanitary state that the city was forced to make its replacement a priority. There was no choice. A plan was conceived to erect a replacement courthouse on a site at the top of Bay Street.

In 1884, the property was purchased for $200,000 and a young Toronto-born architect, Edward James Lennox, was engaged to design a new building and provide all the necessary drawings. That new city hall would have to wait. However, having spent two thirds of the original appropriation of $300,000 just to purchase a site, it was obvious there wasn't enough money left for a building. There'd have to be a change in plans. After much discussion, officials finally agreed that the only way out of the dilemma was to merge two projects into one and erect a combined courthouse/city hall. This idea would allow them to tackle the taxpayers for the extra money that would be required. The citizens concurred with this reasoning, something they might not have done had they known the ultimate financial outcome. Nevertheless, with additional funds approved by a series of bylaws, the new building began to grow. And as it did, so too did its cost. By the time Lennox's magnificent new municipal building was ready for opening, the taxpayers had shelled out an astounding $1,650,000. But even that figure wasn't final, since all the costs had yet to be accounted for. In fact, by the time architect Lennox's long-simmering dispute over the fees that were still owed him had been settled, the total cost of the courthouse/city hall had reached an astounding $2,271,615, more than seven times the original $300,000 estimate.

Caricatures above the main door of Old City Hall depict a city councillor with his tongue lolling out and architect Lennox.

With the opening of Toronto's new municipal building, the young Toronto architect had become the toast of his profession. People came from all over the continent to witness his work; his talents were praised far and wide. In succeeding years he went on to design industrialist George Gooderham's King Edward Hotel and millionaire entrepreneur Sir Henry Pellatt's Casa Loma. But it was his work on Toronto's City Hall that was to continue to give him grief. Lennox's interim bill for $61,615 was paid without hesitation. But when he requested additional payments for things such as "extras and trips" (to investigate other similar projects), "court house plans not accepted" (i.e. work done before it was decided to combine building uses), "site supervision" (Lennox took over when the contractor on the job fell behind in the work schedule), and "remainder of design fee," he was rebuffed by city officials. In an attempt to recover these costs, Lennox sued the city for $208,000. The litigation went on for more than a decade before the unhappy architect finally settled for a mere $60,000. Caricatured in the frieze work at the top of one of the pillars flanking the main entrance are some strange-looking people, many with grotesque looks on their faces. Councillors-of-the-day who constantly battled with the architect, I'm told. And that other guy? One very unhappy Edward James Lennox.

September 12, 1999

Building Up Our Tallest Structures

Over the years, one of the claims made by city officials was that Toronto was home to the tallest buildings in the entire country. Such declarations can be traced back to the early 1890s, when Edward James Lennox's new eight-storey Farmers' Hotel opened at the southwest corner of King and Jarvis Streets. This unique structure later became the Bristol Apartments. Following its demolition the site was occupied by a Supertest gas station and later by an auto tire sales outlet. Today it's the site of a new condominium. In 1897, the "tallest building" title was transferred to the Independent Order of Foresters' new Temple Building that was erected on the northwest corner of Richmond and Bay Streets. This behemoth scraped the sky at ten storeys.

"Where can we possibly go from here," Torontonians asked. Well, the answer wasn't long in coming with the arrival in 1905 of the fifteen-storey Traders Bank Building at the northeast corner of Yonge and Colborne streets. Later renamed the Bank of Hamilton Building, this structure, now an office building, still stands at 61-67 Yonge Street. That "tallest" title was passed on once again in 1913 with the opening of the new Canadian Pacific Building at the southeast corner of King and Yonge. Two years later, the twenty-storey Royal Bank at the northeast corner of the same intersection captured the title, while at the same time upping the honours by becoming the "tallest in the British Empire." The

A 1922 view looking east on St. Clair Avenue towards the Avenue Road corner. The Methodist Deaconess Home is behind Peter Witt streetcar 2644 operating on the Avenue Road route (that ran from Front and Yonge to St. Clair and Caledonia via Yonge, Bloor, Avenue Road, and St. Clair). To the extreme left of the photograph is Deer Park Presbyterian (now United) Church.

The same view today, with the old church dwarfed by the Imperial Oil Building, at one time the highest building in Toronto, towering over it.

TRADERS BANK BUILDING, TORONTO.

The Traders Bank at Yonge and Colborne Streets, at one time the tallest building in the city, was important enough to be the subject of this souvenir postcard. This bank building was surpassed in height by the new CPR Building at Yonge and King, which in turn was outdone by the Royal Bank, then by the new Bank of Commerce Building at 25 King Street West.

Royal Bank held onto its place in the Empire's record books until 1931, when the Bank of Commerce Building just along the street at 25 King Street West captured the title. In 1965, Montreal's forty-five-storey Place Ville Marie became the tallest in the country, a ranking that was short-lived due to the opening of the TD Centre, a fifty-six-storey black monolith, in 1967. Six years later, Commerce Court topped the TD Centre by a single floor, making it the country champion. In 1975, another bank building, this time the Bank of Montreal's seventy-two-storey First Canadian Place at the northwest corner of King and Bay, became the tallest in the country. And so it remains.

One city building that had a brief fling at being the highest in Toronto will come as a surprise to many. Located on the south of St. Clair Avenue West, between Yonge Street and Avenue Road, is the Imperial Oil Building. It was built in the mid-1950s at a time when the Bank of Commerce on King Street West was the city champ in terms of height above the sidewalk. However, because the new Imperial Oil Building stood on the rise of land north of the ancient Lake Iroquois shoreline (which becomes particularly obvious when travelling Yonge Street or Avenue Road north of Davenport Road) the top of the nineteen-storey building was actually above the top of the thirty-four-storey Bank of Commerce. To be more precise, the former is 241 metres (790

The CPR Building, southeast corner of Yonge and King Streets, 1913.

feet) above sea level, the latter, a mere 228 metres (750 feet). As a result, from the time the St. Clair building opened until the first TD Centre tower was completed nearly a decade later, visitors to the Imperial Oil Building's observation deck could view the sights from the highest point in Toronto.

September 19, 1999

*The Scotiabank building seen to the right of the streetcar in the 1999 photo was demolished in 2002. A new condominium is planned for this site. Another condominium is in the works to replace the Ministry of the Environment building that towers over the old bank.

Bank of Commerce Building, King Street West — Toronto's tallest building for many years.

The Genesis of University Avenue

In a recent column, I described the origin of one of Toronto's major north-south arteries, Jarvis Street. Readers will recall that this street began back in the mid-1820s as a dirt driveway connecting the residence of Samuel Peters Jarvis (which was located near today's Shuter-Jarvis intersection) with Lot Street (now Queen Street) to the south. At about the same time and a few "chains" to the west (a "chain" being a surveying term used to describe a length of sixty-six feet), today's broad University Avenue was also beginning to take shape. It too originated as a driveway. This time the drive would connect Lot Street with a proposed Anglican college to be known as King's College that would be erected on land now occupied by the Parliament Buildings.

In 1829, land for the new school and its "grand" driveway (plus a narrow strip of land connecting with Yonge Street to the east, which has evolved into College Street) were conveyed to the college authorities by prominent citizens of the Town of York, a little community that just five years later would be elevated to city status and renamed Toronto. The new King's College finally opened in 1842 and eight years later became part of the newly federated University of Toronto. Some time later, the university relocated to a site further to the west and the former King's College building was abandoned for a time before being resurrected as the University Hospital for the Insane. In 1886, the building was demolished and the present Parliament Buildings erected on the site. Some have suggested that not all the inmates found new accommodations.

For a time, what is now referred to in its entirety as University Avenue was actually made up of two distinct thoroughfares: the private

Looking south down University Avenue, about a century ago.

The same view today. The statue of Sir John A. Macdonald, the Dominion of Canada's first prime minister, appears in both views.

driveway known as the College Avenue (for King's College) and, abutting it to the east, a narrow public street called Park Lane. Both streets ended at Queen Street. Over time, these two streets were combined into one under the name University Avenue; in 1931, it was extended south to Front Street.

The photos accompanying this article both look south down the College Avenue, a.k.a. University Avenue, from the Parliament Buildings. The time span between the views is approximately one century.

September 26, 1999

Increasing traffic led to the extension of University Avenue south of Queen to Front. The project took place in the early years of the Great Depression, and the workers were glad to get the work and the money.

Harvey's Began a Beautiful Thing

Regular readers of this column will be aware of my interest in the origins of street, place, and company names. For example, the Yonge in Yonge Street honours Sir George Yonge (a close friend of our city's founder, John Simcoe); Hamilton, as in Hamilton, Ontario, recalls pioneer land owner George Hamilton; while the supermarket known as Loblaws recognizes one of its founders, Theodore Pringle Loblaw. And then there's John Harvey. Who is John Harvey, you ask? Read on.

Without intending to confuse the reader, the John Harvey story actually starts with Rick Mauran. He was a young man from Montreal whose father had introduced a new type of restaurant, called Chalet Bar-B-Q, to the citizens of that fair city. Sometime in the mid-1950s, Mauran brought a similar concept to Toronto and opened it under the name Swiss Chalet on Bloor Street West, across from Varsity Stadium. It was the city's first Swiss Chalet restaurant in what is now a chain of more than thirty city-wide. A short time later, Mauran took a big chance and opened a Swiss Chalet in far-off Buffalo, New York. One day, while visiting his American venture, Mauran called in at Pat's, a small one-man hamburger joint across the street from his new restaurant. Instead of the hamburgers being grilled, Pat cooked them over charcoal, a brand new concept as far as the young Canadian entrepreneur was concerned. And boy, were those hamburgers delicious!!

Above: The original Harvey's restaurant on Yonge Street south of Richmond Hill soon after it opened in 1959.

Left: A newspaper ad that ran during the summer of 1959 for Harvey's Used Cars on the Danforth.

Always on the lookout for new ideas, Mauran immediately decided to establish a similar outlet in Ontario. He acquired a site on the east side of Yonge Street, just south of Richmond Hill, on which he built a small drive-in restaurant. So far, so good. But now he had a problem: what to call the place. At that time, Henry's was the name of a popular New York state chain of restaurants, so why not try something similar? Something like, say, Humphrey's. But Mauran was running short of money, and a new sign with that many letters was just too expensive.

Here's where John Harvey enters the picture. While Mauran was pursuing his dream in Richmond Hill, John Harvey was in the process of closing his used car lot at 2300 Danforth Avenue. He'd put everything up for sale, including the sign out front. Somehow Mauran found out about that sign, bought it, and hauled it up to the Richmond Hill site. With a couple of minor alterations, Harvey's Used Cars became Harvey's Hamburgers. Today, forty years after the first Harvey's opened at 9741 Yonge Street (where it's still in business), there are 375 Harvey's restaurants nationwide.

October 3, 1999

The Tale of Toronto's Unfortunate Titanic Survivor

Though it happened nearly ninety years ago and was nowhere near the magnitude of the world's worst shipping disaster (approximately 7,700 souls were lost when the German troop ship *Wilhelm Gustloff* was torpedoed by a Russian submarine on January 30, 1945) the story of the untimely end of White Star's elegant liner *Titanic* and the loss of 1,523 passengers and crew still evokes awe and wonder. Several Canadians were among the *Titanic* victims, and although Toronto passenger Major Arthur Peuchen wasn't one of them, his survival altered the major's life so radically that in the years that followed, there were times when he must have felt that it would have been better had he gone down with the ship.

Peuchen, a prominent city businessman, proud officer in the Queen's Own Rifles of Canada, and former vice-commodore of the city's prestigious Royal Canadian Yacht Club, was a frequent traveller to the European continent. Ocean crossings had become routine for Peuchen, so when he learned that the date of his scheduled return trip coincided with the maiden voyage of one of the wonders of the modern age, he took the necessary steps to book passage on the Royal Mail Steamship *Titanic*. At least this time, the crossing would be a little different. He had no idea just how different it would be.

Major Arthur Peuchen (centre) looks happy in this photo taken at a garden party held at Casa Loma. His behaviour changed following the *Titanic* tragedy, however, when his friends shunned him for being a survivor.

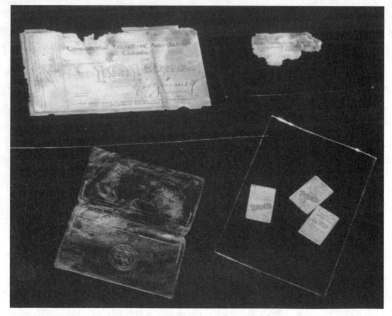

Streetcar tickets and personal papers that were found in Peuchen's wallet, which was recovered from the wreck site decades later.

As all the world now knows, late in the evening of April 14, *Titanic* struck an enormous iceberg, and in less than three hours the "unsinkable" ship plunged to the bottom of the Atlantic. Of the 2,228 souls on board only 705 survived; for better or for worse, Peuchen, who had left his wallet, jewelry, and a collection of stocks and bonds in his cabin on C deck when he left the foundering ship, was one of them. Upon his return to Toronto, and in spite of his pleas that once his yachting experience became known to one of *Titanic's* senior officers he was ordered to assist with the manning of lifeboat #6, Peuchen quickly became the object of scorn and derision. He had survived; hundreds of women and children had not. Edwardian morals dictated that nothing else mattered. It was obvious that Peuchen was nothing more than a coward.

In the days, months, and years that followed, the once popular Torontonian was shunned and was frequently the object of derisive comments. Peuchen's nephew once told me that people would often yell "Peuchen, you bastard!" as the pair walked the city streets. Peuchen's troubles finally came to an end when he passed away at his 105 Roxborough Avenue West residence on December 7, 1929. He rests in Mount Pleasant Cemetery.

Since 1987, RMS Titanic, Inc. has scoured the R.M.S. *Titanic* wreck site and in the process recovered nearly five thousand artifacts, including the wallet that Peuchen left in his stateroom when the word came to abandon ship. In that wallet were some still-legible printed documents and three Toronto Railway Company streetcar tickets. Initially they were incorrectly identified as TTC tickets, an impossibility since the Commission didn't come into existence until nine years after the sinking. The TRC was a private company that provided streetcar service for Torontonians from 1891–1921.

October 17, 1999

Our Subway Keeps Rolling Along

It's hard to imagine Toronto without its fast and efficient subway system, which is presently made up of two distinct, yet fully integrated routes (Yonge-University-Spadina and Bloor-Danforth). The system utilizes a total of 638 subway cars operating over 56.4 kilometres of track and serves a total of 66 stations. This, of course, is a far cry from Toronto's first subway line, a 7.36-kilometre stretch of the present Yonge line that opened in late March 1954 with 100 cars and serving 12 stations between the terminals at Union Station and Eglinton Avenue.

Work on the Yonge subway was first proposed (in a slightly modified form) early this century, but it wasn't until September 8, 1949, that work officially got underway on what would be Canada's first subway. One of the photos accompanying this article shows the public ceremony that was held at the corner of Yonge and Wellington Streets on that September day fifty years ago. Participants were the lieutenant-governor of the day, Ray Lawson, and Toronto mayor Hiram McCallum, while the master of ceremonies for the big event was none other than Winnipeg's own Monty Hall, at that time an employee of CBC Radio, who went on to become one of the corporation's pioneer TV hosts before moving stateside. Also taking part in the proceedings (perhaps because there was nobody else around that particular day) was French movie actress Corinne Calvet, who was in town promoting her new movie.

The official start of the Yonge subway construction fifty years ago at the corner of Yonge and Wellington Streets. This view looks north on Yonge Street to the Wellington corner. The facades of buildings to the left of the view are now part of BCE Place.

Back in the 1950s, Toronto's new subway made it onto souvenir postcards such as this one.

Four years, six months, and twenty-two days after this ceremony, another official event took place, this time uptown at the new Davisville subway station, where Ontario Premier Leslie Frost and

Mayor Allan Lamport threw the switch to get the new Yonge subway up and running. Interestingly, on the day construction work on the Yonge line began, a story appeared in the *Toronto Telegram* that gave an update on the province's plans to construct a pair of new "superhighways," one to be known as the Toronto By-pass across the north end of the city (now Highway 401) and the other the Toronto-Barrie Highway (promoted by some as the Huronia Highway, a term that never caught on). The latter is now identified as Highway 400. Highways and subways continue to vie for government funding.

Located in front of 62 Laing Street in the east end of Toronto is a small cottage that research tells us was erected in 1873 when that part of the city was described as "wilderness." In front of the little cottage is an ancient maple tree that, legend has it, was the inspiration for Alexander Muir's stirring song *The Maple Leaf Forever*, which for a time was Canada's unofficial national anthem. The story describing the song's origin goes like this. In the fall of 1867, Muir, a teacher in the small community of Leslieville (in and around the present day Queen and Leslie intersection) was searching for something to be the subject of a tune he had composed for a patriotic song contest being sponsored by the Caledonia Club of Montreal. One day, while Muir and his friend George Leslie (a pioneer settler of the area and the man for whom both Leslieville and Leslie Street are named) were out for a walk, they passed under the ancient maple and one of its leaves fell and clung tenaciously to Muir's overcoat. Try as he might, Muir couldn't dislodge the leaf. "There's the subject for your song, Alex," said Leslie, "the maple leaf, forever." Muir agreed and quickly composed additional lyrics (some of which have since fallen out of favour) and entered his new song in the competition. The young schoolteacher's song came in second, earning Muir a prize of fifty dollars. But there's more to the story. Prodded by friends to have his work printed in sheet music form, Muir had one thousand copies printed at a cost of thirty dollars. Unfortunately, sales were miserable (he sold a mere four dollars' worth). In the end, his prizewinning composition had only earned Muir twenty-four dollars.

October 24, 1999

Dancing Down at the Pier

Recently, I was fortunate enough to attend the new musical *Forever Swing* at the Ontario Heritage Foundation's beautiful Winter Garden Theatre in downtown Toronto. As I listened to a variety of the songs made famous by the American big bands of years ago, I realized what it must have been like to live back in the 1930s and '40s when swing was all the rage. Toronto had many fabulous dance halls; places like the Palais Royale, Columbus Hall, Club Esquire, Top Hat, Embassy, Mutual Arena, and the Silver Slipper up the Humber were just a short streetcar ride away.

Sharp-eyed readers will notice that I've left out one of the most popular of them all, the Palace Pier, located just west of Sunnyside at the mouth of the Humber River in Etobicoke Township. That's because while the Pier eventually did become one of the city's most popular dancing destinations, for a long while the place didn't know what it wanted to be. In fact, when first proposed in 1928 by several businessman operating as Provincial Improvement Corporation, the new Palace Pier was described as a "year-round amusement enterprise" that would feature a fifteen-hundred-seat theatre, a huge games arcade, an enormous ballroom, a bandstand, plus a variety of shops and eating places. All this would be packed into a pier stretching more than a third of a mile out into Lake Ontario. But things didn't go smoothly,

A stubby Palace Pier juts out into Lake Ontario at the mouth of the Humber River. Also seen in this c.1960 view are (far right) the Stelco factory, the Village of Swansea (north of the Stelco factory), and the Queensway and Lakeshore Road bridges.

The Palace Pier was more than just a dance hall, as these ads confirm.

Torontonians had plenty of other dance halls to choose from.

The story and photographs of the ill-starred Palace Pier are affixed to one of the structure's footings, which can still be found at the foot of Palace Pier Court near the mouth of the Humber River.

and after years of litigation, what Torontonians actually got was a much abbreviation version of the original concept. Instead of stretching that third of a mile out into Lake Ontario, what was actually built was only three hundred feet in length, and what was worse, no one knew what to do with the truncated pier.

When the new attraction finally opened in the spring of 1941, it was as the Strathcona Palace Pier roller rink. It was also known as the Queensway Ballroom, then the Humber Pier Ballroom. It was as a dance hall that the place thrived, and before long all the great American bands were signing up to play Toronto's major dance hall, which had reverted back to its original name, the Palace Pier. For more than two decades dancers flocked to the mouth of the Humber to hear and dance to the best of the big bands. Sadly, Toronto's most popular dance hall came to a fiery end on January 7, 1963.

October 31, 1999

Leaside Long Ago

It's been almost two years since the "new" City of Toronto came into being as a result of the amalgamation of the former cities of Toronto, North York, Etobicoke, Scarborough, York, and the Borough of East York into one homogeneous entity. It seems the jury is still out on whether the undertaking can be classified an unqualified success. One thing that didn't change with the creation of the new city on January 1, 1998, was the public's refusal to eliminate the names of the expunged communities from their vocabulary. As a result, we still hear people describing themselves as residents of North York, Etobicoke, or Scarborough.

Interestingly, the same thing happened back in 1966 when the original Municipality of Metropolitan Toronto was streamlined from thirteen to just half a dozen participants. Many people residing in the seven neighbourhoods that were officially obliterated back then (Long Branch, Mimico, New Toronto, Forest Hill, Swansea, Weston, and Leaside) still refer to their communities using the original titles. Swansea and Weston are particularly adamant about retaining their names, as is the former Town of Leaside. Most residents in that part of our new city continue to refer to themselves as Leasiders.

While on the subject of Leaside, this community's name honours pioneer settler William Lea, whose father had emigrated from England to our city (then called York) in 1819. Eventually, Lea Senior acquired

William Lea (1814–1893), pioneer settler for whom Leaside was named, is buried in the little cemetery adjacent to St. John's, York Mills Anglican Church.

two hundred acres of rolling land south and east of today's busy Bayview and Eglinton intersection, where he established what in time became a highly successful farm. Several years later, William began farming land adjacent to that of his father, where he soon built himself a house that he called "Leaside." When the fledgling CPR laid its track through the Lea farm in the early 1880s, it perpetuated the name of the house by calling a station on its new West Toronto–Peterborough line "Leaside."

The actual Town of Leaside emerged thanks to entrepreneurs William Mackenzie and Donald Mann, who had built Canada's third transcontinental railway, the Canadian Northern. In 1912, the pair decided to create a new town site northeast of Toronto on some one thousand acres of farmland they had purchased from various landowners, including members of the Lea family. Leaside attained town status in 1913, and in recognition of its first mayor, Randolph McRae, two of the town's main streets were given the names Randolph Road and McRae Drive.

Industry was important to the fledgling community, with one of the first, Canada Wire and Cable, purchasing a large parcel of land on the east side of a dirt trail called Laird Drive in 1914. With a war raging in Europe, the company quickly opened a factory nearby, where shells to feed the hungry Allied guns were turned out by the hundreds of thousands. Some three years later the federal govern-

Do you know what this strange structure was used for? It stands on the now abandoned Canada Wire and Cable property on the east side of Laird Drive, where it's been a curiosity for the past few years. If you know what it was used for, write me c/o the *Sunday Sun*, 333 King Street East, Toronto, M5A 3X5.

ment built one of the city's first airfields on the plateau of land east of the ammunition factory, and it was here that many young pilots got their initial flight training. Sadly, several died in the attempt. Soon after the "war to end all wars" ended, the Durant Motor Car (and later Dominion Automobile) Company moved into several of the old buildings and began turning out a variety of vehicles, including the Durant, Star, and Frontenac automobiles as well as Rugby trucks. The problems associated with the Great Depression eventually brought an end to all car and truck production in Leaside. The Canada Wire and Cable Company continued manufacturing operations at the Leaside site for many years until it too decided to move to more modern facilities. Recently, all of the ancient buildings on the sprawling factory site were demolished and the land cleared. Can redevelopment of this valuable land be far in the future?

November 28, 1999

*As a result of my request for assistance on the purpose of this structure I received several replies. John Bennell, Jack Gauley, Joe McQuade, Dave Rawling, Charles Sultana, and George Nutter, all of whom worked at the nearby Frigidaire plant and had at different times toured the old Canada Wire and Cable factory, confirmed the building was a "vertical extrusion tower." It was here that bare copper-wire cable manufactured in the nearby factory reeled up one side of the tower, where it was given a hot rubber coating in a special machine located at the top of the structure. The coated cable then cooled as it descended the twenty-one metres (seventy feet) to the main floor, where it was collected on huge reels. By performing the entire operation in a vertical structure the company was able to save on valuable floor space.

Not long after this column appeared, the tower, which some thought would be retained as a community landmark, was demolished. A big box mall development now occupies the site of the tower and factories.

The House That Arthur Built

Construction of Casa Loma, Sir Henry Pellatt's rambling residence located north of the busy city on Mr. Joseph Well's hill (thus the term Well's Hill that's still in use), began in 1911. When it was finished two years later, the "castle" boasted ninety-eight rooms. While Casa Loma's superstructure was taking shape, not far to the west, near the dusty Oakwood Avenue–Rogers Road intersection, Arthur Weeden was busy finishing off his own "castle" at 128 Day Avenue. However, unlike the two years it would take to build Casa Loma, Weeden's construction schedule would be much, much shorter, for instead of constructing a home with nearly a hundred rooms, Weeden's would have just three. When these two gentlemen finally moved into their respective homes, Casa Loma was unquestionably the city's largest, while that of Mr. Weeden was its smallest.

The reason for Pellatt's decision to build such an opulent residence was so that there would be an appropriate place for his king and queen to stay if and when they came a-calling. According to an article in a July 1931 edition of the *Evening Telegram*, Weeden, a well-known building contractor in the Earlscourt district, had a much different answer when asked why his place was so small. The lot on which he would build his small residence (and I emphasize small, for it's only seven feet, seven inches wall-to-wall) had originally been the driveway

"CASA LOMA". TORONTO. CANADA

Postcard view of Sir Henry Pellatt's magnificent residence, Casa Loma.

128 Day Avenue, Toronto's smallest house.

for the house to the south. When York Township work crews arrived one day in 1912 to lay sidewalks, they neglected to cut a curb for this driveway. Weeden seized the opportunity to claim the land, on which he quickly erected a new, albeit small, house. Obviously, building bylaws back then were somewhat different.

Toronto's second-smallest house at 383 Shuter Street is a whopping eight inches wider than the city's smallest.

Today, Pellatt's castle is a very popular tourist attraction, but no one has actually lived there since a market value reassessment prompted Sir Henry to move out in 1923. On the other hand, 128 Day Avenue continues as a residence. Its present occupants are Edson and Patricia Sobrinho, a pleasant young couple who came to Canada three years ago from their native Brazil. At first, they lived with his parents in the little house, but they have had it all to themselves for the past three years. By the way, some have suggested that the house at 383 Shuter Street in the heart of the city is Toronto's smallest. According to my tape measure, the Shuter Street residence is actually eight inches wider than the one at 128 Day Avenue.

December 5, 1999

The Way We Could Have Been

As the 1900s come to a close, it's interesting to speculate on the way Toronto might look today if certain proposals of yesteryear had actually been completed. The list of new roads, high-speed expressways, and jumbo buildings planned but not realized is lengthy. In this column, I'll look at just a few of the more interesting twentieth-century projects that failed to materialize.

By the mid-1960s, the city's main airport, which had opened nearly three decades earlier and was originally named for the nearby village of Malton, was in need of major expansion. One idea was to build a new airport south of the city on a structure floating atop Lake Ontario. Access to and from the facility would be by shuttle train, helicopter, and hovercraft. The *Sun*'s Andy Donato (back then an artist with the *Toronto Telegram* newspaper) drew the accompanying sketch in 1968; it shows Toronto's proposed floating airport, complete with the arrival and departure of several Concorde-type passenger jets. Unlike the Concorde, Toronto's floating airport didn't get off the ground (or, in this case, atop the water). Not only that, but even after years of dickering, we still haven't been able to build a rail transit route to the airport we do have.

Another non-starter was a 1971 proposal that would have seen the world's tallest building, a $120-million, 140-storey, triangular-shaped

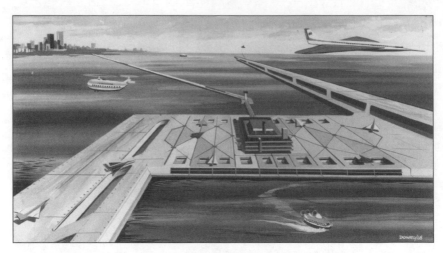

Andy Donato's 1968 concept for Toronto's new floating airport. Note the city skyline at the top left of the sketch.

John Maryon admires a model of his proposed skyscraper, which, if built, would have been the world's tallest building.

structure, erected here in Toronto on a site that had yet to be confirmed. Nevertheless, London, England-born engineer-turned-developer John Maryon said in an interview that he had the financial backing from Australian and European interests for his project. When asked about the proposed structure's unusual profile, he stated that the triangular shape would lessen the impact of wind loads on the 503-metre (1,650-foot) building, which, with its 600-foot communications mast, would have topped the yet-to-be-thought-of CN Tower. As to just where Maryon planned to erect his new building, the architect suggested the site of the Eaton's College Street store (now College Park) would, in his opinion, be ideal.

December 19, 1999

Take a Turn Through Toronto

The morning of January 1, 1900, had dawned cold and grey in a much smaller, much more modest City of Toronto. And while many of the city's two hundred thousand or so citizens stayed up late to celebrate the arrival of another new year, the hoopla and excitement were at a minimum. Not even the fact that the 1800s had been surpassed by the 1900s generated much interest. In fact, the closest thing to a real New Year's Eve story in the January 2, 1900 edition of the *Evening Telegram* was a brief report filed by the paper's police court correspondent in which he revealed that a mere four citizens had been arrested by the police for being drunk in a public place while welcoming in the new year. The cases were heard in the courtroom of what we now call Old City Hall. The first two were immediately dismissed. The third involved Mary Brown, an elderly woman without a fixed address. She was more than happy to accept a sentence of three months. It was winter, and a cell in the Don Jail was certainly warmer than any Toronto street.

Then the judge came to Jennie Hackett. "Yes, I was drunk," asserted Jennie. "But I have an excuse. It's my first time this year." Amused by the accused's quick wit, the judge let her go with a warning. Justice had again been served. And just what did Jennie Hackett's Toronto look like? While the accompanying birds-eye sketch was done in 1878 (it was tipped into *Toronto Illustrated*, now an extremely rare book), the view

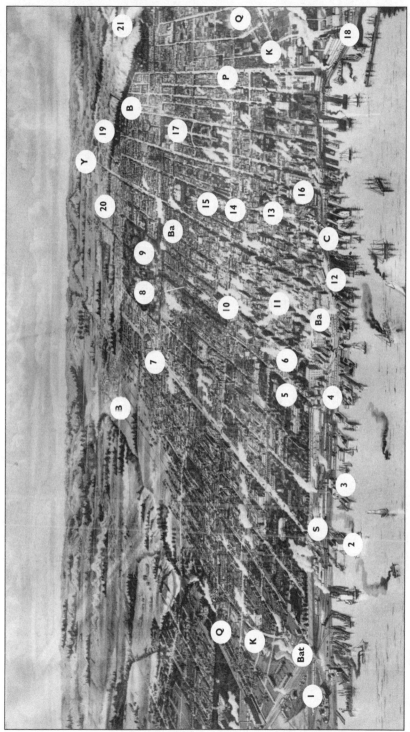

See key on following page.

gives us a pretty good idea of how Toronto appeared a century ago. We're looking north from a vantage point over Toronto Island. An asterisk indicates the landmark is still standing. If demolished, the structure presently occupying the site, or part of the site, is shown in brackets.

Happy New Year!!

January 2, 2000

KEY

1 Old Fort* (now known as Historic Fort York)
2 Grand Trunk Railway grain elevator (CN Tower)
3 City Water Works (SkyDome)
4 Second Union Station (office building south side of Front Street West, opposite University Avenue)
5 Government House, King and Simcoe streets (Roy Thomson Hall)
6 St. Andrew's Presbyterian Church*
7 Knox Theological College*
8 University College*
9 Queen's Park*
10 Osgoode Hall*
11 Mail Building (First Canadian Place)
12 Grand Trunk Railway station (Hummingbird Centre)
13 St. James' Anglican Cathedral*
15 St. Michael's Roman Catholic Church*
16 St. Lawrence Hall and Market*
17 Horticultural (Allan) Gardens*
18 Gooderham and Worts distillery*
19 Rosedale
20 Village of Yorkville
21 Don River and Valley

Streets
Bat Bathurst
Ba Bay
B Bloor
C Church
K King
P Parliament
Q Queen
S Spadina
Y Yonge

Time and a Clock Keep East Ticking

One of the most frequent questions I receive from readers of this column has to do with the Queen Street East bridge over the Don River — more specifically with the story behind the clock and sculptured text that appear at the west end of the bridge. Before I answer the question, though, let's first take a look at some of the earlier bridges that crossed the Don in this part of the city. Back then the thoroughfare was actually known as the Kingston Road, not an unreasonable title since this pioneer trail connected the young Town of York (Toronto's name prior to 1834) with the bustling community of Kingston 260 kilometres to the east.

One of the first references to a bridge being erected over the Don in this vicinity appears in an 1827 newspaper. Because of its bad state of repair, the editors took the opportunity to question who was actually responsible for its upkeep: the local authorities or the province? This would appear to be the same bridge over which British troops retired and which they then set on fire following the capture of York by American forces in April 1813. So important was the bridge that it was immediately repaired, only to be set afire once again twenty-four years later during William Lyon Mackenzie's unsuccessful attempt to overthrow the Family Compact-controlled provincial government. Though badly damaged, it was repaired and lasted until a new wooden bridge was erected in 1851.

The Queen Street East low-level steel bridge over the Don River was erected in 1878. This view, looking west, was taken in 1900.

The 1878 low-level bridge was replaced by this, the present structure, in 1912. Note the clock and text referred to in the article.

Heavy rains in early 1878 caused the Don to overflow, and this bridge too was wrecked. Later that same year a new steel structure was in place, and it stood until 1912, when the present bridge was built. A steady stream of heavy vehicles (such as the TTC streetcar in the photo) have made it necessary to strengthen this structure many times since then. Now, back to the original question: why the clock and the text? In the mid-1990s the Queen/Broadview Village Business Improvement Area held a public art competition with a view to creating identifiable symbols for the neighbourhood that would also enhance the area's image. The winning submission, called "Time and a Clock," is the creation of local resident Eldon Garnet. His work actually comprises three elements: the clock and accompanying text on the bridge; more text inlaid in the sidewalk at the busy Queen/Broadview intersection; and a quartette of poles that are located on the north side of Queen Street at Empire Avenue, each of which flies an inscribed stainless steel pennant. All three refer in some way to the subject of time. As for the text over the bridge, the statement "The River I Step In Is Not The River I Stand In" is a variation of an assertion by one of the lesser known Greek philosophers, Heraclitus (534–475 BC), who, the Internet Encyclopedia of Philosophy reminds us, once scribbled, "You cannot step twice into the same river." Being a student of science, I'm afraid the rest of the analogy escapes me.

January 9, 2000

Turn of the Century — 100 Years Ago

In my column of January 2, 2000, I wrote about how little attention was paid to the arrival of the year 1900 (a year that actually marked the end of the nineteenth century). As that column related, only four city drunks were corralled by the police on January 1, 1900, making it one of the quietest New Year's Days in the young city's history. It wasn't until the twentieth century dawned a year later (January 1, 1901) that Torontonians got really caught up in things.

One special event would be the welcoming in of the new century with the inaugural ringing of City Hall's new set of bells. For some reason the trio of bells and the clock mechanism had not been ready in time for the official opening of the hall back on September 18, 1899. In fact, research has subsequently revealed that the necessary components hadn't even been ordered from the English manufacturer until September 13, 1899, five days before the hall opened. Nevertheless, by the end of 1900 all the components were in place, and at exactly one minute to midnight on December 31, 1900, the bells began to ring as Toronto embarked upon the twentieth century.

That century was only twenty-two days old when word arrived that Queen Victoria had died. Her passing was keenly felt in Toronto, where most of the population had known no other monarch but Victoria. Two of the city's major downtown thoroughfares (Victoria and Queen) had

Drawing of the proposed Queen Victoria memorial statue that was to be located in a new park south of the then-new City Hall, 1901. Obviously, nothing came of this grand scheme.

been named in her honour, as had Queen's Park, so designated during the visit of her son Edward, Prince of Wales, to Toronto as part of his 1860 North American tour. Originally it had been known simply as University Park. Even Victoria's husband had been well regarded in our city and was honoured in the naming of Albert Street. Soon after her passing an idea began to circulate that would have seen a huge statue of the late queen erected in a park to be created opposite the then-new City Hall. In the accompanying sketch we can see the massive memorial, which would have been framed on the west by the old Temple Building (on the northwest corner of Bay and Richmond streets; it was also Toronto's first "skyscraper") and by the new City Hall to the north. While nothing further came from this grand scheme, Victoria did get further recognition a couple of years later with the unveiling of sculptor Mario Raggi's somewhat smaller bronze and granite creation in front of the Ontario Parliament Buildings.

January 16, 2000

Falling Victim to Killer Flu

A choo!!!

Excuse me!!! Well, it's that time of year once again, and it seems as if everyone has the simple sniffles, a full-blown cold, or a serious case of influenza. But as bad as our present-day population may feel as they hack and wheeze through the next few weeks, advances in the various fields of medicine will hopefully result in the vast majority of victims recovering without side effects any more serious than a major dent in the wallet for those boxes and boxes of Kleenex. Unfortunately, that wasn't the case back in 1918, when countless millions worldwide succumbed to the effects of the great influenza pandemic that swept the globe in the second half of that year. Most often identified as the Spanish Flu (flu from inFLUenza), it was also known as Singapore fever, Flanders grippe, Blitz Katarrh (German for "lighting cold"), and a number of other descriptives. Identification with Spain probably arose from the fact that during the Great War Spain remained neutral, a fact that allowed that country's news media to give more prominence to the disease than the media of other countries, where the illness also raged but censorship kept its effects on the war effort secret. Spain's neutrality also made her very unpopular amongst the warring factions. As a result, the belligerents certainly had no hesitation in having the disease identified as the "Spanish" influenza.

Military Base Hospital, Gerrard Street East, where many military personnel died during the October 1918 Spanish influenza epidemic.

Closer to home, researchers have estimated that between thirty and fifty thousand Canadians died of the disease, a substantial figure in relation to the nation's 1918 population of approximately eight million. Not only were the effects of the disease felt within the young country's well-populated cities, as one would expect, but small outposts such as the Cartright camp in distant Labrador were also devastated. The death rate in this isolated community rose to a staggering 25 percent. Here in Toronto, the city's various newspapers kept a close watch on the progress of Spanish influenza as it crept up on the city. Toronto was then a city of nearly half a million and already tired of death notices that for the past four years had identified its young warrior citizens, who had been dying by the hundreds overseas. The first influenza cases were reported in the local papers in September 1918, with the first death attributable to influenza reported in the October 2, 1918 edition of the *Evening Telegram*. Poor John Hamilton of 10 Magee Street was only thirty-two when he succumbed to pneumonia, the frequent and all-too-often fatal result of influenza. As the month progressed, more and more cases were reported, and soon the wards in the city's public and private hospitals were overwhelmed with influenza cases.

Some of the most virulent cases were to be found in the Military Base Hospital on Gerrard Street East between Sackville and Sumach

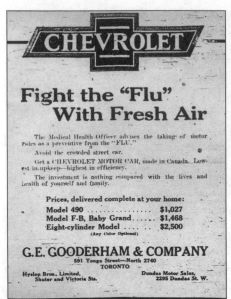

Some Toronto companies suggested a new car or their nourishing bread might help prevent influenza. The flu had a major impact on Bell telephone, which asked its customers to be tolerant.

streets. This rambling old building had served for years as the city's principal hospital, until the new Toronto General opened on College Street in 1913. It was to this ancient structure that the young men stationed at the various military camps in and around the province were taken when they became sick. The building became so overcrowded that wards had to be opened in the cold and draughty attic. Toronto's Mayor Church was soon blasting the military authorities for allowing the camps at Petawawa and Niagara-on-the-Lake to remain open when heated buildings at the Exhibition grounds were available. The military was slow to react, and many soldiers were to die, not on the battlefields of Europe, but right here in Toronto.

That's not to say that only citizens and soldiers were stricken. So too were doctors, nurses, and other caregivers, and soon the call went out for volunteers to help look after the sick, especially mothers with children living in houses where food and fuel were in short supply. The response to the plea was heartening.

October 23 would be a record day in Toronto. On that day, a total of eighty-seven citizens passed away from influenza or its complications. When the epidemic finally subsided in early November, officials crunched the numbers and estimated that 150,000 people, or 30 percent of the city's population, had been stricken. Of that number more than 1,400 died. It was the first and only time in the city's history that burials had to be conducted on Sundays, just to keep up.

January 23, 2000

Sound Fit for Castle

Occupying a place of prominence in Casa Loma's Great Hall is an immense theatre organ. And while the castle may be approaching its ninetieth birthday, the organ has been a fixture at Casa Loma only since February 1974. So where did it come from? Here, briefly, is the fascinating story of the Casa Loma organ. When multi-millionaire Henry Pellatt was developing plans for his new residence on Well's Hill, a place we know today as Casa Loma, he arranged to have a three-manual, thirty-rank Franklin Legge organ included as one of its many features. Unfortunately, both the building's owner and the organ were in the castle for only a short period of time. We know that Pellatt moved out in 1923 due in great measure to being "market value re-assessed" (property taxes rose from $600 annually in 1914 to $12,000 a year just ten years later), but just when the original organ vanished is anyone's guess. In a recent conversation with theatre organ historian Alan Lowry (whom I hadn't spoken to in over ten years and who called me as I was writing this article — scary!!) he told me that while he wasn't sure when the organ vanished from the castle, he did know that it went to the studio of radio station CKNC on Davenport Road, then to a CBC studio on Jarvis Street, and is now regularly played in a Roman Catholic church in Kingston, Ontario. That then is the brief story of the castle's first organ.

A few of the many workers who built Casa Loma take time out to pose for the cameraman on April 24, 1913.

Casa Loma's mighty Wurlitzer organ was originally heard in Shea's Hippodrome on Terauley (Bay) Street in downtown Toronto.

The story of the one that's presently in the Great Hall is better known. Soon after Pellatt moved into his uptown castle in 1913, two young theatre entrepreneurs from Buffalo, New York, Mike and Jerry Shea, began developing plans for their new 1,500-seat Toronto playhouse downtown. Shea's Hippodrome would open in 1915 on the west side of Terauley Street, just opposite Toronto's City Hall. (Today, Terauley Street is Bay Street and City Hall is now Toronto's Old City Hall.) Seven years after the theatre's glitzy opening, a marvellous new Wurlitzer organ was installed. Many readers will recall such performers as Horace Lapp, Kathleen Stokes, and Quentin Maclean seated proudly at the console as the organ rose majestically from beneath the stage. The marvellous sounds that cascaded from its hundreds of pipes easily filled the interior of the cavernous playhouse. Soon after the Hippodrome closed in late 1956 (the theatre site would eventually be occupied by the eastern part of Nathan Phillips Square), the Wurlitzer was moved to Maple Leaf Gardens, and there it remained until 1964. In that year, it was purchased by the Toronto Theatre Organ Society and placed in storage. A full decade would pass before the former Hippodrome organ was played again, this time in Henry Pellatt's castle on the hill.

January 30, 2000

Time Running Out on Old Meters

Once again someone has taken away another of the poor, beleaguered motorist's God-given rights, the right to park at a meter in downtown Toronto after evening rush hour and all day Sunday for free. Not only have the hours during which payment is required been lengthened ('til 9:00 PM on weekdays, 1:00 PM to 9:00 PM on Sundays!), but the amount charged per hour has also increased to two dollars an hour. Be warned! Check the meter! Check your bank account!

Interestingly, when the idea of installing parking meters on the streets of Toronto was first proposed by the civic works committee back in 1936 (just one year after the very first meters appeared on the streets of Oklahoma City), Toronto City Council voted eleven to five against the idea. They wanted nothing to do with what many referred to as "automobile hitching posts." In fact, several of the councillors had a more pragmatic answer to the ever-increasing problem of what do to do with drivers who wanted to park downtown: build more off-street parking lots and prohibit on-street parking altogether. They reasoned that without parked cars clogging the main streets traffic would flow more smoothly, thereby lessening the congestion that even in the 1930s was becoming a major problem in the city's core. The anti-parking-meter faction remained successful for another fifteen years. Then, on February 19, 1951, after a four-

In 1953, Mayor Alan Lamport tried to explain why his choice, the Red Ball meter, was a better choice than that of city council, the Park-O-Meter. It was one of the few arguments the feisty "Lampy" lost.

Left: New "pay and display" meter.

hour debate, City Council approved a one-year "trial" installation of meters in an area bounded by Front, Jarvis, Dundas, and Simcoe streets. The maximum charge at each meter would be twenty cents for one hour. All revenues accrued from the meters were to go to pay the $100 cost of each meter, with the surplus used to fund the construction of off-street parking facilities. The first of the 1,100 meters went into operation on Albert and James streets, just outside City Hall, on February 25, 1952.

The next year the legendary Alan Lamport got into a yelling match with several councillors and the *Telegram* newspaper over his desire to have the Red Ball model parking meter (manufactured by the Parker Pen Co.) installed on Spadina Avenue instead of the Park-O-Meter model (invented by David McCowan, whose ancestors are recognized in McCowan Road) that had already been adopted by council. Some councillors even suggested that the president of Parker Pen was a close friend of Mayor Lamport, which had prompted "Lampy's" position on the matter. Lamport vehemently denied both the allegations and "the alligators" (a statement that was to become a documented Lampyism). However, his motion to use the Red Ball meters on Spadina was defeated. Interestingly, no meters all were to be installed on Spadina for the next few months. When they did appear, Lamport must have been looking the other way, for they were Park-O-Meters. Today, the Toronto Parking Authority still looks after some 14,500 parking meters across the city. Recently they introduced a new type of parking control device. Known as the DG Classic, this state-of-the-art machine is manufactured in France by the Schlumberger Company. A variation of this type of "pay and display" machine has been in use in off-street lots for almost a decade. Thus far, nearly 160 of these state-of-the-art machines, costing approximately $14,000 each, have been installed, with many, many more planned. Each unit is solar powered, accepts both cash and credit cards, and has a wireless connection with a central monitoring station to ensure it's always operating properly. Each unit serves a parking area that, depending on the size of the vehicles using that area, accommodates up to 10 percent more vehicles than when individual meters served the same area.

In the two weeks following the introduction of parking meters in early 1952, a little over $1,600 was generated. This year, metered parking revenues will bring in nearly $11 million.

February 6, 2000

Where There's Smoke, There's Fire

When the Toronto Police Association announced it was starting a fundraising campaign with contributors receiving either a bronze, silver, or gold window sticker depending on the amount pledged, little did the association realize just how big a can of worms it had opened. The media jumped on the sticker part of the campaign and planted in the public's mind the perception that some police officers might take the colour of the sticker into account when in the process of issuing a ticket for a driving infraction. Having worked on a number of projects with members of the Toronto Police Services, their professionalism makes that thought laughable. Nevertheless, the perception that it might play a part had been planted, and soon this possibility was being played for all it was worth in the media. Before long, it was the police against the public.

Actually, my first thought, once I had digested and discarded the media's suggestion that there might be some improprieties inherent in the Association's sticker program, was the way that those stickers could be compared to something called fire marks that were issued by privately owned fire insurance companies many centuries ago. First issued in Britain in 1667, these fire marks were small metal plaques issued by fire insurance companies to clients who would in turn would affix them to the front of a house, office, or factory as proof that the property was, in

The "British America" fire engine was presented to the young City of Toronto in 1837 by the insurance company of the same name. This company is now part of Royal & SunAlliance Canada.

fact, insured by the company whose name appeared boldly on the plaque. The purpose of this plaque was simple. Up until the time fire fighting became a municipal responsibility, that service was usually provided by the privately owned fire insurance companies themselves. When an alarm was raised, several of these brigades would respond. The fire mark was used to identify whether the structure on fire was a client of one of the attending fire companies. If it wasn't, the fire fighters would wait until the client's own company arrived. That was, of course, unless a next door neighbour's place was in peril and it happened to display an attending company's fire mark. Then the boys would go to work. Obviously, the fire mark gave the client preferential treatment — much as, some suggest, a gold sticker on a car windshield would.

While the fire mark idea was popular in both Britain and the United States, it never had the same impact here in Toronto. Local fire insurance companies did issue them, but more for advertising purposes than anything else. That was because the city had extremely dedicated volunteer firemen and actually paid individuals to haul water to the site of a blaze: three dollars for the first to arrive, two dollars to the second, one dollar to the third, and fifty cents to the fourth. As a result there was no need for local insurance companies to have their own firemen, although one or two did donate fire-fighting equipment. It wasn't until 1874 that Toronto established a paid, full-time fire department.

Oh, that sticker idea. Thankfully, saner heads eventually prevailed, and the police got back to the difficult task of serving and protecting our great city without various coloured stickers getting in the way.

February 6, 2000

Love of Wheels Goes Way Back

The public's love affair with the automobile is certainly not a new phenomenon. You just have to look at the expressions on the faces of these turn-of-the-century motorists parked in front of the Alexandra Palace apartment hotel on University Avenue, just south of College, for proof. And that relationship continues to this day, with thousands eager to visit this year's Canadian International Autoshow, now underway at the Toronto Convention Centre on Front Street West.

Car shows have a long tradition here in our city, starting in early 1906 with the first public showing of what skeptics were still calling the "horse-less carriage" in the old University Avenue Armouries. It wasn't long before car shows had started to become regular features at the annual CNE. Initially these shows were held in the Transportation Building at the west end of the grounds, a large structure that had been constructed in 1909 specifically for the exhibiting of cars, trucks, and an even newer mode of transportation, the aeroplane. The public's adoration of new cars and trucks culminated in a larger building being opened at the east end of the Exhibition Grounds in 1929. It was here in the new Automotive Building that Canada's first National Motor Show was presented in March 1932. Some of the now-vanished models displayed at that show included McLaughlin-Buick, Hudson, Willys-Knight, De Soto, Packard, La Salle, Studebaker, and Essex. In fact, the first car to be purchased by a

A quartet of pioneer car buffs parked on University Avenue c.1904.

Cars became so popular that the CNE added a million-dollar building in which to show them off. When the new Automotive Building appeared in time for the 1929 CNE it was described as the largest building devoted to exhibiting new vehicles anywhere in the world. This photo shows the 1953 edition of General Motors' "Motorama" in the Automotive Building.

Canadian hero General Sir Arthur Currie (1875–1933).

member of the public attending the show was an Essex. As an added attraction, the show featured afternoon tea dances (with music provided by Bob Cornfield and his band) and supper dances (these featured Luigi Romanelli's Orchestra), as well as two lavish floor shows each and every evening. General admission to the show was fifty cents. The National Motor Show, as well as the car show held during the run of the CNE, continued for many years; it wasn't until 1967 that Exhibition officials finally abandoned the car show. This action was necessary because the fair's dates had been moved ahead in time, while new car introduction dates became progressively later in the year. No one wanted to see year-old cars.

The history of what is now known as the Canadian International Car Show goes back to 1974, when its premiere event was presented at the International Centre. That show required about 100,000 square feet of exhibit space and welcomed just over 80,000 visitors. This year's show covers over 550,000 square feet and anticipates a ten-day attendance of more than a quarter of a million guests.

I see there's another plan to change some Toronto street names in an effort to lessen post office confusion and misdirected emergency vehicles. Here we go again. In March 1944 a report in a local newspaper quoted the Postmaster of the day demanding something be done about the confusion caused by the duplication of Toronto street names. Sound familiar? I wonder if changes will occur any quicker this time around? Actually, many years ago there was an attempt to change the name of one of our major

Lord Lansdowne (1845–1927) of Lansdowne Avenue fame.

city thoroughfares. It had nothing to do with confused postmen. No, it had to do with a burst of nationalism. In 1917, while the First World War was raging and thousands were being killed, Lord Lansdowne, who had served as Canada's governor-general from 1883 to 1888, and the man for whom a street in Toronto had been named, sent a letter to the *London Times*. In it he strongly urged the allies to sue for peace. For many, this suggestion was the meddling of a traitor. In fact, many British subjects living on or near Toronto's Lansdowne Avenue were so infuriated by the proposal that they demanded city officials show their disdain for Lansdowne by changing the thoroughfare's name to Currie, thereby honouring a real Canadian hero, General Sir Arthur Currie, who had just been appointed commander of the battling Canadian Corps. Obviously, that proposal failed. However, there are still a couple of Lansdowne avenues (including the one near Glencairn and Caledonia). Who knows, perhaps they'll try to change the name again.

February 20, 2000

Toronto Has History of Thinking Big

At the end of the month, city council will be asked to give its approval to permit Toronto to enter its name in the competition to host the 2008 Olympics. Will that approval be given? Will Toronto win? And if we do, will Torontonians be better off for having been the host city? Stay tuned! Well, at least one thing's for sure. If Toronto is successful and we do become the host city, this place just won't be the same. The changes, not to mention the bills that'll pour in, will be enormous.

Actually, if practice counts for anything we're a shoe-in. Over the years Torontonians have put forward dozens of grand (and expensive) schemes. Some of the ideas that never went forward, or should I say into the ground, involved a plethora of new City Hall and Civic Square projects, the first dating as far back as 1911. Then there was the monstrous Eaton Centre plan of the early 1960s, the one that would have seen our Old City Hall demolished and the entire block bounded by Queen, Yonge, Dundas, and Bay littered with a multitude of high-rise structures and a massive shopping centre. Or what about the Toronto Union Terminal and Commercial Building project of 1911? If this thing had gone ahead the entire area bounded by King, Yonge, Queen, and Simcoe would have been covered by a twenty-storey structure with a gross floor area of 40 million square feet. That project surfaced while municipal officials were discussing a new Union Station for

A model of Buckminster Fuller's 1968 scheme for downtown Toronto and its waterfront shows the Gardiner Expressway still in place, as are the CN Roundhouse (extreme left) and next to it the John Street water pumping station. Where, oh where, are they going to put the Tower and SkyDome?

Toronto, so the developers threw in a huge railway depot down in the building's basement as a kind of bonus. Perhaps the grandest scheme of all was the ill-fated Metropolitan Centre project that, in its original form, would have seen the destruction of Union Station and virtually every square inch of real estate between Front Street and the Gardiner from Yonge to Bathurst covered with buildings of every shape and size. This billion-dollar project was just too much for the public to swallow. The CN Tower is the doomed scheme's legacy.

Down on the waterfront schemes also came and went. Among them were such things as an offshore floating airport; Craig, Zeidler, and Strong's Harbour City; and, as recently as 1981, Barton Myers's "The Embankment," which was to be located at the foot of Spadina Avenue. In 1967, a plan called "The Bold Concept" emerged that would have seen the entire waterfront between the CNE grounds and Cherry Beach, including Toronto Island, totally transformed. Part of this transformation would have been the provision of a series of new parks complete with Olympic Games (!!) facilities. Remember, this latter component, a place to hold the Olympic Games, was put forward thirty-three years ago!

One of the most spectacular proposals for a "new" Toronto was put forward in 1968 by American inventor and architect Buckminster Fuller. Instigated by John Bassett, publisher of the *Toronto Telegram*, "Project Toronto" would have cost more than one billion dollars. The plan had University Avenue extended south into a new neighbourhood that would boast thirty-five thousand citizens living and working on land reclaimed from Toronto Bay. The new street would have been flanked on one side by a three-thousand-foot-long enclosed galleria, complete with shops, cafes, and hotels, and on the other by a four-hundred-foot-high Crystal Pyramid office complex. In addition, the CNE grounds would become home to a new university, with the annual fair relocated to Downsview Airport, where a complex in which the Olympic Games could be held would also be built. Fuller's "Project Toronto" was in reality simply an exercise in future thinking, but note that it too featured provisions for the coveted Olympic Games.

Toronto will be soon getting a new museum. This one, to be known as the Toronto Aerospace Museum, will be devoted to the history of aviation and aerospace activities that have taken place in and around Toronto and will be located in one of de Havilland Canada's aircraft hangars on the former Downsview airport property. One of the first artifacts at the new museum is the Lancaster bomber that for many years slowly deteriorated on its concrete pedestal on Lake Shore

Boulevard just south of the CNE grounds. It, along with several other aircraft, has recently found a new home at the soon-to-open museum. One of the many ambitious projects put forward by museum officials is a plan to build a full-scale replica of the Arrow #25203, the third of five such aircraft to roll off Avro Canada's assembly line out at the old Malton Airport. Arrow #25203 spent a mere thirteen hours in the air prior to the cancellation of the project on February 20, 1959, and the subsequent unconscionable destruction of all five of these remarkable aircraft. To assist with the mammoth job of reproducing what has become a icon in Canadian aviation history, the museum is looking for volunteers to work on the engineering and assembly aspects of the venture as well as individuals or companies that might wish to supply equipment and/or materials. Of course, money to help finance this challenging undertaking would also be welcomed. To learn more phone the Toronto Aerospace Museum at 416-638-6078 or check out its web site at www.torontoaerospacemuseum.org.

February 27, 2000

*The Toronto Aerospace Museum did materialize, and work is well underway on both the Lancaster and the Arrow replica.

Oh, For Those Gas Price Wars!

I guess just about everyone remembers his, or her, first car. Mine was a 1949 Morris Minor I purchased the summer I worked between school years with Ontario Hydro. Several years later, I opted for something newer, and only slightly more reliable, a 1958 Hillman Minx. Having spent the greater part of my still young life in one school or another, when I finally graduated from Ryerson and got a job, I decided to blow the bundle on a brand new 1965 Ford Fairlane two-door Sports Coupe. Now, when I say I blew the bundle, having just started to work I really didn't have much of a bundle to blow. But thanks to Yarmila (who would become Mrs. Mike Filey three years and three cars — a '67 Ford Mustang, '67 Dodge Monaco, and a '68 Mercury Montego — later) I was able to come up with the required down payment to at least order the car. I then floated a loan from her family's credit union and soon the Fairlane was mine — mine and the credit union's, that is.

Now the reason for this brief historical look at my car-buying youth is to simply point out that all the time I was buying cars, both old and new, the least of my worries was coming up with the money to fill the gas tank. Why things are different today I'm really not sure, since in relative terms, today's gas costs about the same as it did forty years ago. Perhaps concerns about the price of gas were fewer back then simply because there were so many companies to choose from. Unlike today,

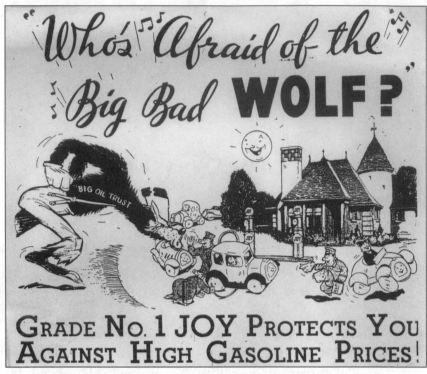

1938 newspaper ad showing Joy Oil (and its service station attendants dressed as the three little pigs) protecting Toronto motorists from big oil trusts, here represented by the big, bad wolf. Plans are presently underway to try to retain a former Joy station on Lake Shore Boulevard and convert it into a convenience store for the new community planned for the abandoned Stelco site nearby.

when those choices are limited to less than a half-dozen or so, back then we had a list that included, along with Esso, Sunoco, and Shell, companies like Fina, Texaco, Supertest, Cities Service, Regent, Joy, B-A (soon to become Gulf), and White Rose. In the early 1960s, even Canadian Tire was getting into the gas retailing business. This abundance of choices no doubt helped prompt the gas wars that always seemed to be going on somewhere in the city. Often the price of a gallon would drop and continue to drop as one station tried to better his neighbour. In addition, there were always better prices at the so-called "discount" or no-name stations scattered around town. A two or three cent per gallon difference translated into significant savings, back when you could fill the tank for less than five bucks. You know, I can still remember filling up with thirty-cents-a-gallon gas at the little

Regent station on Lake Shore Boulevard just west of the Humber River, right next door to Brooker's drive-in restaurant, a place famous in its own right for the fabulous twelve-inch (forget that 30.48 centimetre nonsense) hot dogs. Once, during a trip to Buffalo, I filled up with something called "Good Gulf" at 29.9 cents a gallon at a time when American and Canadian dollars were almost at par.

The optimism afforded by hindsight suggests that back then fuel was almost a gift. Then there was that friendly little upstart in the petroleum business, a company called Joy Oil. Many readers will remember this company primarily because of its cheap prices, promotional gifts, and miniature chateaux-like stations. Joy Oil was the brainchild of Margaret Austin, whose husband, real estate magnate Herbert Austin, had organized the Sunny Service Oil Co. in Detroit in 1928. Sunny Service sold gas at discount prices and quickly became profitable, much to the chagrin of the major American oil companies. Following Herbert's death, Margaret brought his company into Canada, changed the name to the Joy Oil Co., and in 1937 began selling a gallon of regular gas for 14.8 cents, plus 6 cents provincial tax. Naturally, this upset the local companies, whose posted price was twenty cents a gallon plus the tax. A few years later Joy Oil ran into trouble with city officials who refused to issue permits allowing the construction of above-ground storage tanks in the Eastern Terminals District, even though the large oil companies had similar tanks nearby. Joy Oil also upset the status quo by opening some stations on Sundays and in doing so was fined numerous times. In spite of continual opposition to its pricing and marketing techniques (opposition from everyone except the car driving public that is), Joy Oil flourished until a variety of insurmountable difficulties eventually brought the company to its knees. At one time there were as many as fourteen Joy outlets here in Toronto, and while the company vanished years ago, one of those stations remains at the northwest corner of Lake Shore Boulevard and Windermere Avenue in the pleasant little Toronto community of Swansea.

March 5, 2000

The House That Was Chorley Park

One day several weeks ago, I received a phone call from a reader wondering if I could answer a question that came up while he and a few guests were sitting around playing a game of bridge. The question had to do with something in Toronto called Chorley Park, and while a couple of the more senior participants present had heard of the place, no one could give any specific details. In fact, he said, the inability of anyone around the table to come up with the answer had put a major damper on the card game. Well sir, here is the answer, albeit a couple of weeks too late to save the card game.

Though the word "park" is in its title, most people who remember Chorley Park will probably remember it as a fifty-seven-room French-chateau-like structure located not far from the top end of Glen Road in north Rosedale. Though the residence may have been called Chorley Park by most people, its official title was Government House, and as such it was home to a succession of five provincial lieutenant-governors from its opening in 1915 until, as a cost-cutting measure, Premier Mitch Hepburn closed it as an official residence in 1937. Government House was known by the name Chorley Park because it had been erected in the middle of a large grassy area known as Chorley Park, a name selected by the original landowner, John Hallam, to honour his hometown of Chorley, Lancashire, England.

This Government House, at the southwest corner of King and Simcoe Streets, preceded Chorley Park.

Government House in Chorley Park replaced the previous Government House, which was located on the site of today's Roy Thomson Hall.

Same view through the residence's one-time entranceway, 1999.

Born there in 1833, Hallam immigrated to Canada while still a young man. He arrived in Toronto in 1866 and established a hide, wool, and leather business. In addition to being a successful business-man, Hallam served for many years as a city alderman, in which capac-ity he was instrumental in starting the city's public library system. He was also a founder of what we now know as the Canadian National Exhibition and in his leisure time became one of Canada's best-known horticulturalists. To showcase his talents, Hallam established a fine summer home, which he called Chorley Park, on the west bank of the Don Valley in north Rosedale and surrounded it with thirty-three acres of beautiful gardens, rockeries, and walkways. The park soon became a destination for citizens and visitors to Toronto alike. Upon Hallam's death in 1900, Chorley Park was added to the city's inventory of open spaces, and it was here that Government House was built in 1915.

Following the closing of Chorley Park (the house, not the green space), the crumbling residence was put to series of uses (a military convalescent hospital, barracks for the RCMP, and a home for Hungarian refugees) before being demolished by the city in 1961.

March 19, 2000

Remembering Canada's First War Dead

L ocated in the centre median of University Avenue, just steps north of the Queen Street corner, is a powerful soaring memorial that is seen by thousands every day. And you know, I'd be willing to bet that of those thousands who drive and walk by it, only a very few would be able to describe just what this imposing memorial commemorates.

I guess that's not surprising given the limited amount of Canadian history taught in our school system. Students probably know more about the American Civil War or the history of major league baseball than they do about the South African War, a conflict in which, for the very first time in the country's young history, Canadian troops fought, and died, on foreign soil.

Though the war didn't erupt until mid-October 1899, the seeds for the conflict had been sown in 1814 when British troops occupied the Cape of Good Hope, causing great anxiety for the ethnic Dutch Afrikaners (Boers) who had settled the area years earlier. Britain continued with its strategy of territorial acquisitions, and as it did, the Boers continued to grow more and more concerned. The situation went from bad to worse in 1886 following the discovery of gold in the Transvaal, an event that prompted a large influx of prospectors, mostly from Great Britain. The animosities between the powers came to a head on October 12, 1899, when the Transvaal and Orange Free State declared

South African War Memorial cornerstone laying ceremony, September 11, 1909. Lieutenant-Governor Hendrie with trowel.

Memorial nearing completion, late summer 1909. Note that the figure atop the column is not yet in place and University Avenue is still beautifully tree-lined.

South African War Memorial today.

war on Great Britain. The Boers, whose troop numbers at the time greatly exceeded those of the British forces, had been well equipped by their ally, Germany. As a result, the initial stages of the war went poorly for Great Britain, prompting a call to her Dominions for assistance. Canada was quick to respond, "for the integrity of the Empire."

That's not to say that all Canadians believed that the young nation should get involved. The French Canadian populace saw Britain's involvement in South Africa as meddling, pure and simple, similar to the interference it continued to effect here in Canada. On the other hand, most English Canadians couldn't wait to help the mother country in her hour of need. Ultimately, 7,368 Canadians served in South Africa, seeing action at places such as Paardeberg Drift, Johannesburg, Diamond Hill, and at the Relief of Kimberley and Mafeking. Of that number, 264 paid the supreme sacrifice, some to enemy action, most to the ravages of enteric fever.

The war ended on May 31, 1902, with the signing of the Treaty of Vereeniging. Even as many of the Canadians were making their way home, plans were being formulated for some sort of permanent memorial to honour those who would never return. Unfortunately, and for a variety of reasons, funds were hard to come by, resulting in another seven years passing before the cornerstone of Toronto sculptor Walter Allward's magnificent monument was to be tapped into place. Another glitch in the evolution of Toronto's new war memorial occurred when Lord Beresford, who was scheduled to do the honours on September 11, 1909, telegraphed from Northern Ontario, where he had spent a few days fishing, reporting that he would be unable to be present because he had missed the train. At the last moment Ontario's Lieutenant-Governor George Hendrie stepped in, and the ceremony went ahead.

On May 24 of the following year, General Sir John French, commander of the British cavalry during the war, dedicated the 1,000-ton, 130-foot-high memorial "in memory of the Canadian soldiers who fought and fell in South Africa." Since then, the memorial has been moved twice, once in 1949, when the University Avenue centre median was relocated, and again ten years later during the construction of the University subway.

March 26, 2000

Toronto's "International" Intersection

You know, I've wanted to visit Australia ever since I discovered that it too has a place called Toronto. For one reason or another I've never made that trip. Someday, perhaps. In the meantime, however, I can at least get that "Aussie" feeling by simply driving through the Bathurst Street/Lake Shore Boulevard intersection. What the heck am I talking about, you ask? Well, those who traverse that busy intersection are no doubt aware that there's a major streetcar track installation project underway. When the work is finished (the trackwork portion sometime in early to mid-April, the overhead wire installation soon thereafter) streetcars will be able to operate from Union Station direct to Exhibition Place (and return) via Bay Street (underground), Queen's Quay, Bathurst, and Fleet streets.

Now here's where the Australia part of my story comes in. The switches and crossovers in the intersection are a product of the Davies and Baird foundry in Melbourne, Australia. So as your car or truck dances over the intersection, you'll enjoy a little feel of Australia. To be completely accurate, within a couple of weeks the Bathurst/Lake Shore/Fleet intersection will be truly international in scope. It'll have "tee" rail from Cape Breton, Nova Scotia; girder rail from Germany and Pennsylvania; steel joint bars from Woodstock, Ontario; hardwood ties from Quebec; and electric switch machines from North Carolina.

Looking north on Bathurst Street over the Lake Shore/Fleet Street intersection from the Esso gas station lot on the southwest corner, October 1935. Note the Loblaw's warehouse on the northeast corner.

Same view, March 2000. It's still an Esso station, and while it's now self serve, the old garage structure still stands. In the distance, the Gardiner Expressway soars over Bathurst Street, and part of that Loblaw's warehouse is now a food bank.

The early history of this particular intersection is interesting if not ancient. That's because up until 1917 this part of the city was underwater, the intersection under discussion being the site of the old Western Entrance into Toronto Harbour. As ships grew in size this entrance was deemed unsafe, and a new entrance, the present West Gap as it's called by some, was built and opened to navigation in 1911. By 1917 the old gap had been filled in, and over the next few years the Toronto Harbour Commission laid out the east end of its modern four-mile-long Boulevard Drive (now called Lake Shore Boulevard West) on the newly reclaimed land. The Bathurst Street part of the intersection came into being in 1931 following the city's realignment of the bridge over the railway tracks south of Front Street (the bridge formerly ran in a southwesterly direction) and subsequent extension of the thoroughfare due south to connect with the Boulevard Drive and another newly constructed street, Fleet, so named to honour the Royal Navy's "Grand Fleet," a prominent force during the First World War.

The TTC first laid track on this part of Bathurst Street and on the new Fleet Street in the spring of 1931. Steel for that job set the TTC back $1,237. Materials for the present work cost $455,000. Thanks to the TTC's Brian Longson for details on the current project.

April 2, 2000

Downtown Devastation

With all the talk these days about removing the Gardiner Expressway (which, while under construction during the late fifties and early sixties, was regarded as one of the most significant projects the city had ever undertaken) and spending millions to redevelop hundreds of acres of land along the city's waterfront, it's hard to believe that ninety-six years ago this coming Wednesday something happened that many predicted would end Toronto's chances of ever becoming a great city. To historians that event has become known as "the Great Toronto Fire."

The evening of Tuesday, April 19, 1904, was cold and blustery. Winds had been clocked at thirty miles per hour from the northwest, and light snow fell on an almost deserted downtown Toronto (most citizens having retreated from the chilly streets to the warmth and comfort of their homes). Then, just minutes after the bells in the five-year-old City Hall clock tower had struck the hour of eight, a patrolling police constable noticed flames shooting into the night sky from the elevator penthouse atop the Currie Neckwear factory at 58 Wellington Street West, a four-storey brick structure just steps, and a couple of narrow lanes, west of Bay Street. The narrowness of these lanes would have a great deal to do with the speed with which the flames would spread and the enormous amount of devastation that was to ensue. The officer ran

Dates on the posters confirm the year of the photo as 1908, and buildings along the south side of Front Street, between Bay and York, still lie in ruins four full years after the fire. This indicates just how slow the recovery of this area, and other nearby parts of the devastated city, was. The property in the view is now covered by Union Station. In the distance is the waterfront, while to the right are the towers of Toronto's old Union Station.

to the nearest fire alarm box, Box 12 at the corner of King and Bay streets, and rang in the alarm. Within minutes, the first fire apparatus, under the command of Chief John Thompson, was on the scene.

Surveying the situation, Chief Thompson knew instinctively that this was going to be a long night for his crews. The winds whipped the flames into a frenzy, and they easily leapt over the narrow laneways to the east. Within ninety minutes all the buildings on both sides of Bay Street north of Wellington and halfway to King Street were in flames. And still the fire spread. By midnight, all the structures along the west side of Bay and on the south side of Front Street were engulfed. Windswept embers also set several wharves along the waterfront alight, and a number of ships had to be towed from their moorings to the safety of Toronto Bay. Then suddenly the wind changed direction, and the flames swept north up Bay and east along Front. By 3:00 AM, the fire was closing in on the Yonge and Front intersection, where a determined stand made by dozens of fire fighters prevented both the ornate Customs House at the southwest corner and the Bank of Montreal Toronto head office (now the Hockey Hall of Fame) across the street from becoming victims. To the west along Front Street a similar effort by firemen, this time assisted by concerned citizens and a clutch of hotel guests, prevented the ancient and beloved Queen's from total destruction. Earlier, loyal employees of the *Evening Telegram* newspaper, whose building stood at the southwest corner of Bay and Melinda streets (a site now occupied by portion of the plaza at Commerce Court), had helped save their workplace from ruination.

By five o'clock the following morning, flames were still burning throughout an area that covered nearly 20 acres, but the 230 firemen on duty had finally checked the spread of the conflagration. Interestingly, Toronto's 1904 firefighting payroll numbered just 196 men. They were assisted by 36 firemen from fire departments in Kew Beach, Toronto Junction, and East Toronto (then still separate from Toronto), who arrived at various times to lend assistance. This obviously meant that while downtown was burning only a handful of men were left to guard the rest of the city. In addition, the massive amount of apparatus in use was supplemented with fire hose and wagons from the Hamilton and Buffalo, New York fire departments.

The conflagration devastated the commercial heart of the city and raised serious concerns about Toronto's future. Official records reveal that a total of one hundred buildings had been destroyed or severely damaged. Destruction in monetary values topped $10 million (1904 dollars). While no one was killed during the nine-hour blaze, twenty-five fire fighters were injured; the most serious injury was a broken leg sustained by Chief Thompson.

April 16, 2000

Debunking a High Park Myth

High Park is the subject of a myth that seems to go on forever. Many people believe that this marvellous piece of property in the western part of the old City of Toronto was given to its citizens as a gift by the owner, John George Howard. Mr. Howard wasn't quite that virtuous. In fact, what Howard actually proposed back in 1873 was that if the city agreed to pay a down payment of $300 plus a pension of $1,200 per year as long as either Howard or his wife lived, the 165-acre parcel of land would, upon the demise of the last survivor, become city property. In addition, there were a few minor conditions to which the city had to agree. That pension had to be tax-free, and the couple had the right to live in their residence, Colborne Lodge, until their deaths, whenever that might be. As well, the city had to agree to maintain the family tomb (which was, and still is, located just west of Colborne Lodge) in perpetuity and ensure that it received two coats of paint or varnish every second year and that the gate to the gravesite be kept locked at all times. The city would also have to call the property High Park, and the name was never altered even to honour its benefactor, Howard himself. Actually, the city got around that little condition by naming one of the streets leading to the park Howard Park Avenue.

Having received Howard's proposal, council set about examining the terms. Since both John and Jemima were in their early seventies, most

John George Howard, the original owner of High Park.

members felt that all in all this was a heck of a deal. How much longer could they last? All the other conditions were acceptable, and when the vote was taken it carried 13-2. By the way, those two dissenting votes were cast by council members who, having thought long and hard about the proposal, decided that the property was too far outside the city limits of 1873 and therefore of limited use as a public park, either now or in the future. And there is no truth to the rumour that these guys are still on council. The city quickly drew up the necessary documents and everyone sat back waiting until the park could be turned over to the citizens.

Unfortunately for poor Mrs. Howard, she only lived four years after the agreement was signed with the city. Mr. Howard, on the other hand,

In the early 1900s, curling on High Park's frozen Grenadier Pond was a favourite pastime.

remained healthy a good long time, eventually passing away on February 3, 1890, at the ripe old age of eighty-six. By then, the city had paid out nearly $20,000 for the 165-acre piece of property, a not-insignificant sum in 1890. In retrospect, one could consider the whole thing as a rather shrewd business deal on the part of the owner. But let's not be cynical.

Today's High Park is much larger in area than the original Howard farm just described. That's because the original Howard property has been added to on two separate occasions since then. The first addition took place in 1876 with the purchase of the 172-acre parcel to the east from Percival Ridout. In 1930, a 71.8-acre parcel to the west, owned by the Chapman estate, was also acquired by the city and added to High Park. Twenty or so years later this new, larger High Park lost some of its acreage when The Queensway was cut through the southern end of the park. Today, according to official documents, High Park has an area of exactly 398.48 acres. Oh, there's also a story that it's illegal to serve liquor on the Howard property. I wonder if it's OK to serve it on the Chapman or Ridout properties? Just asking.

Many readers may not be aware that for six days, commencing April 27, 1813, American troops marched triumphantly through the streets of our community while the "Stars and Stripes" flew over several of our public buildings. The bloody Battle of York was a sad moment in Toronto's past. The future of both our city and country looked bleak. However, our brave soldiers and their First Nations allies saved the day, and in time the invaders were back across the border where they belonged. To commemorate Toronto's place in the War of 1812, two Heritage Toronto plaques will be placed at Victoria Square Memorial Park, Wellington and Portland streets. The first will be at the Old Garrison Burying Ground and will commemorate the final resting place of many of the personnel and their family members who lived at both Fort York and at the "New" Fort (renamed Stanley Barracks in 1893). The second plaque will honour the Church of St. John the Evangelist, "The Garrison Church," which was consecrated in 1858 and in which members of several of the city's historic militia regiments worshipped. The old building was demolished in 1963.

April 23, 2000

Red Rockets Coloured Childhood

When I was a kid growing up on Bathurst Street, just south of the Bloor Street corner, one of my fondest memories was boarding the modern-looking Bloor streetcar with my mother and brother and then travelling east to Yonge Street, where we'd transfer to the older and bigger Yonge streetcar for the "stop and go" trip downtown to Eaton's main store. Here we'd meet Aunt Peggy, who worked in the store's Beddings and Linen department, where we'd leave our coats, hats, and boots before Mom began to tow us through the rest of the store, searching for things that held no interest whatsoever for us, unless those things happened to be from that enchanted place on the fifth floor, Toyland.

In retrospect, Bloor Street itself was an important part of my young life. At the southwest corner of Bloor and Bathurst was a Loblaw's store where Mom would often send me to buy hamburger. If someone tried to foist the more expensive round steak mince on me I'd have to take it back. Even a few pennies were important. Across the street from Loblaw's was the Alhambra Theatre, my movie theatre. A few years ago someone without a heart had this magic place torn down, and now a Swiss Chalet stands on the site. And just a few stores to the west of the Alhambra was a Kresge's store where they sold rolls of caps for my cap gun. (Wonder if they still have cap guns?) Over towards the Bathurst

An eastbound Bloor streetcar, like the one I used to ride, pauses to let passengers off at the Bay Street corner sometime in the late 1940s. In the background, from left to right, are the Park Plaza Hotel (now the Hyatt Plaza), the recently opened 1,556-seat University Theatre, and the Physicians and Surgeons Building at the Bloor and Bellair corner. And just visible over the rear of the streetcar is a large sign that reads "DANCING" that was in front of the famous Club Embassy.

Street corner was Mr. Singer's cigar store, our closest source of chocolate bars and pop. Next to his place was a Downyflake Donut shop where we would gawk through the window to watch the hot, doughy doughnuts plop out of the mechanical doughnut machine into the hot grease by the thousands. Right on the corner was a Rexall drug store.

Bloor Street was also the street I had to cross every weekday morning and afternoon during my time at Palmerston Public School. While crossing Bloor Street to get to school was obviously OK with my parents, crossing to the opposite corner and wandering away to mysterious points further east and north of the busy Bloor and Bathurst corner was definitely not. I also remember a horse trough at the Bloor and Bathurst corner. Nearby one could often find a little old man playing one of those hand-cranked music machines while a small, dressed-up monkey on the end of a chain raced in and out of the crowd waiting for the streetcar seeking coins from an appreciative audience. I also remember (though this memory is really vague) the opening of a store in a large house at the Bloor and Markham corner. It was run by a young fellow named, let's see, oh yes, Ed Mirvish. Wonder what ever happened to him?

Participant in virtually all of my Bloor Street memories were the shiny red and cream TTC streetcars that roamed both Bloor Street and someplace across the Don Valley called the Danforth. When the streetcar went west it was heading for someone named Jane (I never found out her last name) and when going east it was bound for some foreign place called Luttrell. Recently, the Bloor-Danforth streetcar line became the subject of a new video from the studio of GPS Video. The tape incorporates rare colour film footage taken during the 1950s of scenes along Bloor Street and Danforth Avenue, as well as video of the present Bloor-Danforth subway that replaced the surface cars when it opened on February 26, 1966. A potpourri of 1940s and '50s automobiles makes the video that much more interesting. In addition, informative narration is provided by a former Bloor streetcar operator, Bill Hood, and by the video's producer, Ray Neilson.

April 30, 2000

Sunday Sports Not New

It was on this very day fifty years ago that fans got to witness the first-ever professional Sunday baseball game in the city's long 116-year history. That event, which was actually a double-header, featured the city's beloved Maple Leafs confronting their International Baseball League opponents the New Jersey Giants (Leafs vs. New Jersey, where have I heard that combination recently?) at the old "Fleet Street flats" down near the Toronto waterfront. Unfortunately, the results of that pair of games turned out to be a major disappointment for the majority of the more than eighteen thousand fans in attendance. The home team lost both, the first 9–5 and the second 4–1. Nevertheless, Toronto history was made that day a half-century ago.

Back then, the team's home field was Maple Leaf Stadium, which had been constructed by the Toronto Harbour Commission in 1926 in the traditional open-air, horseshoe-shaped style. It was situated at the foot of Bathurst Street fronting on today's Lake Shore Boulevard, which up until 1960 was called Fleet Street (thus the term "Fleet Street flats"), and cost the Commission a whopping $750,000. The hulking structure was flanked on the east by the aforementioned Bathurst and on the west by the appropriately named Stadium Road. To the south were the huts formerly occupied by Norwegian air force personnel during the first few years of the Second World War, where they lived while

Aerial view showing Maple Leaf Stadium, where Toronto sports history was made on May 7, 1950. On that day the Toronto Maple Leaf baseball team played on a Sunday, and it was legal.

training at the Island airport across the Gap to the south. After the war "Little Norway," as the site became known, was converted to wartime housing. The houses were eventually torn down and the present parking lot was laid out. The stadium itself was demolished in 1968, one year after the ball team folded for lack of fan interest. The Blue Jays came along a decade later and played for eleven years in Exhibition Stadium, which too has been demolished.

Today, a half-century after that first Sunday game, the idea of playing professional sports on a Sunday doesn't faze anyone. In fact, in almost every way imaginable, our modern-day Sunday is indistinguishable from an ordinary weekday. But, as many of our senior Torontonians can attest, that wasn't always the case. A few may remember when tobogganing down the hills at Riverdale Park on Sunday was against the law. In more recent times, the publishing and selling of newspapers on Sunday was illegal (the *Toronto Telegram* tried in 1957 and failed); movie theatre doors were to remain shut on Sunday, as were the doors of most restaurants. If you wanted a good meal in Toronto on a Sunday it was off to one of the hotels. And as for buying gas for the car, forget it. However, as the number of cars and trucks increased a bylaw was enacted permitting one station in an area to open from noon until 5:00 PM. The following Sunday, another station would take its turn. History has recorded that the prime motivator for professional Sunday sports in Toronto was the late Allan Lamport. As part of his bid to be elected to the city's Board of Control for the year 1950, Allan entered the game and successfully made the pitch for Sunday baseball.

May 7, 2000

It Was President's Choice

Of all the subjects I've written about in this column over the past twenty-five or so years, the topic that results in the most reader feedback is the Toronto streetcar and its place in our city's history. For instance, a reader recently wrote to tell me one day when he was just a kid, he lost his streetcar ticket and had absolutely no way of getting back home, miles across town. He sobbed his story to a patrolling policeman, who flagged down a passing streetcar and requested, in an official tone, that the driver take the young fellow to the corner closest to his home. The reader went on to say he has never forgot either the policeman or the streetcar operator who, in combination, saved the youngster from being lost forever. Others remembered when their fathers or grandfathers, who worked for the TTC, would take their offspring to the car barn and allow them to sit behind the streetcar's controls for a few moments. What a thrill! Some recalled riding what was called the "free bathing car," a unique summer service that was operated for years by the TTC and its predecessor, the Toronto Railway Company (TRC). As the hot weather arrived, newspaper ads would magically appear giving the dates of operation and routes for that summer's "free bathing car." This special streetcar would roam the city streets, taking inner-city kids (back then just about everybody was an inner-city kid) to and from waterfront bathing beaches or, in the very early days of the service, swimming holes on the Don River. For a time,

One of the thirty PCC streetcars purchased from the Kansas City, Missouri public transit company in 1957. It is seen here in front of the Granite Club on St. Clair Avenue West. Both the streetcar and clubhouse are no more.

the TRC also ran a summer "baby boat." This was a specially chartered Island ferry on board which many of the city's less affluent mothers, and their babies, could enjoy a free outing on the cool waters of Toronto Bay, well away from the heat and noise of the city.

In addition to affording nostalgic memories for generations of Torontonians, the streetcar has had a much more practical effect on our city. In fact, it can be stated with certainty that the physical growth of our city in the early years of the twentieth century was attributable in great measure to the ongoing expansion of the street railway track system. In fact, when the privately owned TRC refused to service the citizens moving into the outlying areas of Toronto (knowing full well its franchise would not be extended past the due date of 1921), a decision that began to strangle the city, municipal officials stepped in and created the Toronto Civic Railways, which quickly began to construct lines on Gerrard Street East and Lansdowne Avenue as well as out on the Danforth and on Bloor Street and St. Clair Avenue in the city's western "hinterland." Coincident with the arrival of the municipally operated TTC on September 1, 1921, not only were the existing lines integrated and fares consolidated, new routes were soon introduced and, to make that ride even more enticing, the most modern street railway equipment available was purchased.

One such vehicle was developed in the 1930s by the Presidents' Conference Committee (PCC), an organization consisting of the presidents of a variety of North American transit systems, each eagerly searching for a new, more efficient, and safer streetcar. Called the Streamliner, it was the most significant improvement to street railway operations since the changeover from real horse power to electric power, an event that occurred here in Toronto during the period between 1892 and 1894. The TTC introduced the public to the first of its PCC Streamliners during the 1938 CNE, a favourite venue back then for the introduction of the latest in technological developments. These revolutionary new cars were subsequently entered into regular service on the St. Clair route on September 23 of that same year. The PCC went on to serve Toronto's transit riders for a total of fifty-seven years, with the last of this once-ubiquitous model retired on December 8, 1995.

Proud of its heritage, the TTC has recently undertaken to retain and refurbish the last pair of PCCs in its streetcar fleet. Numbers 4500 and 4549 are classic examples of 1951 transportation technology from a time when the city had no subways, no Sunday movies, and no structures taller than the thirty-one-storey Bank of Commerce Building. These historic vehicles can now be chartered. They're perfect for church or service group outings or for transportation to an old-fashioned company picnic in High Park. They also give convention visitors a unique way to explore Toronto. The cars (which seat a maximum of forty-six) can be chartered on weekdays (during non-rush hour periods) as well as in the evening and on weekends. Call the TTC Charter Office at 416-393-7880 for all details.

May 21, 2000

Regiment Salutes Queen Mum

Although the Queen Mother's actual one hundredth birthday isn't until this coming August 4, a variety of celebrations are already underway to help this beloved lady celebrate her extra special day. One such event will take place this Tuesday at Fort York Armoury (east of the CNE grounds) when Canada Post unveils a commemorative stamp honouring the Queen Mother as she reaches this remarkable milestone. Of special interest to Canadians in general, and Torontonians in particular, is the fact that this unique ceremony will be hosted by one of this city's most respected military regiments, the Toronto Scottish, whose Colonel-in-Chief is Her Majesty Queen Elizabeth, the Queen Mother.

This regiment has a long and proud history. The Great War had been raging for less than a year when, on July 1, 1915, the 75th (Mississauga) Battalion, Canadian Expeditionary Force, came into being. By the summer of the following year the regiment was in the thick of the fighting, and by war's end they had participated in every major engagement in which members of the Canadian Corps distinguished themselves. The battalion's losses were a staggering 1 in 5, with a total of 1,049 making the supreme sacrifice. Following the end of the war, the 75th (Mississauga) returned to Toronto, where a huge victory parade was held and the battalion dismissed at a giant gathering held at Varsity Stadium. With the return of peace, it was hard for people to

A bobby-helmeted Toronto police officer stands rigidly at attention as Queen Elizabeth (now the Queen Mother) leaves the presentation stand at Woodbine following the eightieth running of the King's Plate, which was won by Archworth. She's accompanied by A.J. Dyment, president of the Ontario Jockey Club. A few steps behind is King George VI.

believe that anything resembling the recent bloodbath could ever happen again. Nevertheless, as remote as many felt that possibility was, a concerned federal government authorized the re-establishment of the battalion. That was followed on June 8, 1921, by the redesignation of the battalion. Henceforth it would be known as The Toronto Scottish Regiment. In 1937, Queen Elizabeth, wife of reigning monarch King George VI, agreed to become the regiment's Colonel-in-Chief.

Just two years later, virtually all Canadians would come to know their queen, and king, much better during the 1939 Royal Visit to Canada. While it was the couple's first visit to our country, Elizabeth would return many times. On May 22, Torontonians, in huge numbers, had their opportunity to greet George and Elizabeth during the couple's whirlwind visit to the city. Arriving at the CPR North Toronto Station at 10:30 that morning, the pair were driven from one end of the city to the other, visiting City Hall, the Parliament Buildings, Christie Street military hospital, Woodbine race track, and the CNE grounds along

Toronto's City Hall decorated for the Royal Couple's visit on May 22, 1939.

the way. The city had never seen crowds as large as those who lined such thoroughfares as Yonge, St. Clair, Parkside Drive, Lake Shore, Bloor, Danforth, and Woodbine. At one point during the tour, while the King visited the University of Toronto's Hart House, his Queen proceeded to the nearby campus, where she met the officers and men of her regiment, The Toronto Scottish. The newspapers proudly reported that the Queen took the time to inspect every soldier on parade, including the members of the regimental band. During the solemn service that followed, Elizabeth presented the regiment with new colours. Two years later, the regiment would rally around those colours as the nation again went to war — the one most believed could never happen.

May 28, 2000

Helping Our Kids Get Better

Even as you read this column, the sixteenth annual Sick Kids Telethon on CFTO-TV is well underway, and I'm sure doing extremely well, thank you very much. And so it should be, given that the Hospital for Sick Children is such an important part of our community. Last year's telethon raised $4.5 million, bringing the fifteen-year total to more than $41 million. The money raised during this year's event will be used to upgrade or replace the very expensive equipment so necessary to help the little ones.

In addition to being the 16th anniversary of the telethon, this year also marks the 125th anniversary of the hospital itself. It was in the early spring of 1875 that Mrs. Elizabeth McMaster, wife of Samuel McMaster (a successful dry goods merchant and nephew of William McMaster, the founder of McMaster University), unlocked the front door of a three-storey row house at 31 Avenue Street, a small, nondescript thoroughfare long since buried under the sprawling Toronto General Hospital. It would be here that Mrs. McMaster and her co-workers would administer to the medical needs of the city's children. It would, in fact, be a hospital for sick children. The new facility had been open for nearly a month before the first patient arrived at that unbolted front door. Her name was Maggie, and she was all of three years old. The child was in terrible shape when she arrived at the front door of the

Sick Children's Hospital, College St., Toronto, Canada

Telegram publisher John Ross Robertson was responsible for this, the fifth Hospital for Sick Children. This building still stands at the corner of College and Elizabeth streets.

new hospital wrapped in an old coat and carried in the arms of her older sister. Maggie had tripped over a pail of boiling water her sister had been using to wash down the kitchen floor. She had suffered severe burns to most of her tiny body. Though there were several general hospitals throughout the city of 68,000, none was prepared to provide the kinds of special treatment necessary for the successful treatment of sick or injured children. It was this lack of specialized treatment that prompted Elizabeth McMaster to open her new hospital. By year's end, a total of forty-four patients had received treatment at the new hospital. Maggie, by the way, recovered completely and, as the records tell it, eventually moved out west, got married, and lived a pleasant enough life. But the outcome might have been different, a lot different.

Over the years the demands placed on the little hospital kept increasing. A series of larger facilities was acquired, but they were never large enough. Just when it appeared as if Elizabeth's dreams of helping all the needy child would be shattered, along came her white knight, John Ross Robertson. Robertson was the highly successful publisher of the popular *Evening Telegram*. But fame and fortune weren't enough, for he too had suffered the pain of losing a little one. He would see that

I wonder how many postcards like this one were sent to the people back home letting them know how little Joey or Mary was progressing? View c.1953.

Nurses head out from the old Hospital for Sick Children on College Street on their way to the new Sick Kids on University Avenue. The new 632-bed hospital was officially opened on January 15, 1951. A total of 223 patients were moved from the old to the new Sick Kids on February 7.

Elizabeth McMaster's dreams came true. In the early 1890s, he financed and supervised the construction of a new 4-storey, 320-bed children's hospital on a parcel of land just west of the College Street and College Avenue (now University Avenue) intersection, a site not far from the site of Elizabeth's first hospital. And while the city requested that it be called the Victoria Hospital for Sick Children (Queen Victoria was everybody's favourite), that name never really caught on. Everyone simply called it Sick Kids. A half-century or so later, the hospital moved once again, this time to its present site at 555 University Avenue.

June 4, 2000

Toronto's Shifting Waterfront

When it comes to photographs that show just how much Toronto has changed over a relatively short period of time, there are none better at illustrating that fact than the two that appear in this column. The Toronto Harbour Commission (renamed Port Authority of Toronto in June 1999) was established in 1911 in an attempt to bring some order out of the planning chaos that had plagued the city's waterfront for decades. At first staff worked out of rented quarters in a small building at 50 Bay Street before moving into larger facilities at 76 Adelaide Street West. However, when the scope of the Commission's work became fully apparent, Commission officials decided to construct their own office building. And in a gesture that would emphasize the Commission's faith in the future of Toronto's waterfront, officials selected a building site right on the water's edge. To design the new building a local Toronto architectural firm, Chapman and McGiffin, was engaged. Once Alfred Chapman's concept had received the necessary approvals, Toronto Harbour Commission engineers got to work on excavating the site — no simple task, since this part of the waterfront had only recently been reclaimed from the harbour and was not the easiest to build on. Nevertheless, by the late summer of 1917 the building's foundations had been completed and work on the actual structure began. Less than a year later the handsome new $245,000 building was

Surrendered to the British soon after the end of the Great War, the German submarine U-97 and its escort *Iroquois* paid a visit to Toronto on June 11, 1919, where they tied up at the Toronto Harbour Commission Building dock.

ready for occupancy. Being right on the water's edge, the building had a variety of vessels tie up at its front door, an occurrence that seems far-fetched today since this same building is now nearly a quarter of a mile north of Toronto Bay. That apparent anomaly can be easily explained. Soon after the new building was completed in 1917, additional land reclamation took place, and by 1926 the structure, once on the water's edge, was itself now sitting high and dry.

Two of the building's early "visitors" were the German submarine U-97 and its escort, the United States Revenue Cutter *Iroquois*. Just days after the Great War ended on November 11, 1919, the two-hundred-foot-long mine-laying submarine, powered by a trio of 300HP diesel engines, sailed into the Port of Harwich, England, where she was turned over to British naval authorities. Given as a war prize to the United States, U-97 was sailed *across* the Atlantic by an American crew, then taken through the Great Lakes to the American Naval Training Station. One of the stops along the way was the Port of Toronto, where hundreds turned out to see this now not-so-fearsome "sea devil." Another visitor to the THC Building was the Island ferry *Trillium* that tied up at its front door on August 25, 1919. Dozens of city officials and invited guests then boarded the vessel and were transported over to the Royal Canadian Yacht Club, where they witnessed the laying of the cornerstone of the RCYC's present clubhouse by the visiting Prince of Wales. By the way, *Trillium* will celebrate its ninetieth birthday next Sunday.

June 11, 2000

In the year 2000, the handsome Toronto Harbour Commission Building still graces the city's skyline, though in a somewhat dwarfed fashion. Cars now park where ships once anchored.

He Leaves Landmark Legacy

Recently, while visiting friends in the Swansea part of our town, I noticed that one of the community's landmark residences had a For Sale sign on the front lawn. Known as the Gemmell House, the handsome brick structure at 181 Ellis Avenue was built circa 1891 by Alexander Gemmell, a prosperous city boot and shoemaker who had a busy retail store at 104 King Street West. The architect of his new house was his son John, who was also responsible for several other homes nearby as well as many commercial and religious buildings in downtown Toronto.

The site selected for the residence was on a high point of land that had commanding views of both Lake Ontario to the south and Grenadier Pond to the east. This latter body of water delineated (and still delineates) the eastern boundary of the Gemmell property. A contemporary newspaper account, written about the time the Gemmell place was under construction, describes the new house as being one of only three in the entire area. Its neighbour to the south was "Herne Hill," the residence of the Ellis family, one of the first to settle this desolate part of then suburban Toronto. The family name was soon given to what started out as simply a narrow dirt trail through the heavily wooded property. Nearby was the home of William Rennie, a prominent seed merchant whose flower beds on the west bank of Grenadier Pond were a popular area attraction

The historic Gemmell House, 181 Ellis Avenue in Swansea, is up for sale.

Architect John Gemmell designed and lived in the house until his death in 1915.

for years. Rennie Sr. is recognized, as are several other family members, in the name of Swansea's Rennie Park.

John Gemmell, the architect, was born in Scotland in 1851 and came to Toronto with his family at an early age. He first attended the Model School and then went on to Upper Canada College, then still at the corner of King and Simcoe streets in downtown Toronto. Taking an interest in architecture he trained under James Smith, with whom he later formed a partnership. The company, Smith and Gemmell, was one of the most successful in the city, with many Toronto buildings to its

Knox College on Spadina Circle, now a U of T building, is one of Gemmell's best-known creations.

credit, including Knox College (1873–75) and the Church of the Redeemer (1879), both of which still stand, the former on Spadina Avenue, just north of College Street, and the latter at the northeast corner of Bloor and Avenue Road. The present Morningside Presbyterian Church in Swansea is also a Gemmell creation, only this time it exists thanks to a substantial donation bequeathed to the congregation of the community's existing Presbyterian church by the architect in his will. Gemmell went a step further by adding, while taking his last few breaths on his deathbed, a codicil to the will that contained a pencil drawing of what the proposed church floor plan should look like. John Gemmell died on March 28, 1915, and is buried with his father in the Necropolis.

Anyone wishing to learn more about the fascinating history of the Swansea community is advised to contact the Swansea Historical Society, c/o 95 Lavinia Avenue, Toronto, M6S 3H9.

June 18, 2000

Where Have I Heard That Before?

So they're going to build some sort of a railway connection between Union Station and Pearson International Airport. Where have I heard that before? Now, I don't mean to rain on anybody's parade, but that proposal has been put forward so many times I'll believe it when I board that first "Airport Special." In fact, it wasn't long after the federal government killed off the Avro Arrow on February 20, 1959, that someone at Avro announced that there were a number of projects on the drawing boards that could keep their employees busy for years. There was a jet-propelled truck, a sports car, a new type of food vending machine, and — wait for it — a plan to develop a railway connection between Union Station in downtown Toronto and the city's airport out in the countryside, a place still known simply as Malton. The Toronto International designation didn't come into effect until the following year. Oh, in case I went past that date too quickly, the Avro project to connect the railway station with the airport was made fifty years ago!

While on the subject of Union Station, today's magnificent structure (it's magnificent even with those ugly kiosks out front) is the third railway facility in our city's history to bear that grand title. The first to feature the "union," or sharing, of facilities was built in 1855 not far from the present one at the southwest corner of Bay and Front streets and was home to the Great Western and the Grand Trunk railways.

A new, and Toronto's third, Union Station was proposed as early as 1905. It wasn't ready for business for another quarter-century. The fellow in this c.1920 photo had a long wait to catch his train. Regular train service in and out of the new station wouldn't happen for another decade.

Years went by, train traffic increased dramatically, and in 1873 a second and much larger Union Station opened at the foot of today's University Avenue. At first it served just the Grand Trunk, becoming a true Union Station ten or so years later when trains of the new Canadian Pacific rumbled into the place. Then came the present Union Station, although it suffered from the same sort of "hurry up and wait" problems that have dogged the airport–railway station project for the past half-century.

In the case of the new railway station, the problems began immediately following a decree signed by federal government officials ordering the railways to build a new station. The year was 1905. The railways quickly found reasons not to build the facility. The result was that ground wasn't broken for Toronto's new Union Station for another nine years. Even as work progressed another roadblock lay ahead. Government and railway officials couldn't agree on the grade and final location of the tracks leading into and out of the new station. So while the physical structure was ready for trains and passengers in 1920, the track problem kept the doors to Toronto's third and newest Union Station closed for another seven years. Sure, the Prince of Wales performed a ceremonial opening of the station during his visit to Canada in August of 1927, but the whole track fiasco wasn't settled for another couple of years. The end result was that full operations didn't start until early 1930 — twenty-five years after the first orders to build a new station came from Ottawa. So if you're waiting for those recently announced improvements to begin taking shape at Union Station, please don't hold your breath.

June 25, 2000

Postcard view of Toronto's second Union Station, which was in use from 1872 until the present station was fully operational in 1930.

A Dandy Fight with the Yanks

Yesterday, we celebrated Canada's 133rd birthday. And in just a couple of days our neighbours to the south will celebrate their 224th. And while our respective nations have had their differences over the years, for the most part, we've been very good friends. Except, that is, during the period between 1812 and 1814, when things kind of fell apart and our two nations went to war. Now, before I get the purists upset with that last statement, the confederation of Upper and Lower Canada, New Brunswick, and Nova Scotia, with the resulting creation of the new Dominion of Canada, was still fifty-five years in the future when the United States declared war on Great Britain. Throughout the conflict the first two of the aforementioned provinces, Upper and Lower Canada, now known as Ontario and Quebec respectively, were the locations of several major battles that erupted following the declaration of war on Great Britain by American President James Madison on June 18, 1812. The causes of the war were varied. Many Americans still despised Britain over events that had taken place years before during their War of Independence (or Revolutionary War, depending on whose side you were on). In addition, the Royal Navy's continual harassment of American ships, ostensibly to find and remove any Englishmen on board trying to avoid a stint in the King's service, only added to that animosity.

Many were killed during the invasion of York (Toronto) on April 27, 1813. One who was fatally wounded was the American Brigadier-General Zebulon Pike, for whom Pike's Peak in Colorado was named. (Sketch courtesy Dr. Carl Benn, Fort York)

It all came to a head with the outbreak of the so-called War of 1812, or as some called it, President Madison's War. Hostilities lasted until the signing of the Treaty of Ghent on Christmas Eve, 1814. However, without the immediacy provided by today's modern news networks, battles continued to be fought well into the following year. As to who won the war, the answer really depends on whom you ask. The "War Hawks" south of the border anticipated an easy and short conflict. Many of them believed that an invasion of the provinces of Upper and Lower Canada would result in the quick surrender of these British colonies. After all, weren't most of their citizens eager to become part of the young United States of America? Obviously not. And we have the sixty-cent dollar to prove it.

One of the most serious battles of the war took place on April 27, 1813, right here in Toronto, a community that at the time was still just a small town called York. During the occupation that followed the storming of the beach in the neighbourhood of today's Sunnyside Beach, the fort (Fort York) was attacked (with many soldiers on both sides killed

On July 4, 1934, the USS *Wilmington* arrived in Toronto Harbour. On board was the government mace that had been taken during the invasion of the community by American forces in April 1813. Note the two most prominent buildings on the city skyline of the day, the Royal York Hotel (left) and the Bank of Commerce, both of which still stand.

and wounded), several public buildings were burned, the library was looted, and the lives of many of its citizens were put at risk. It could have been much worse save for the intervention of one of York's most prominent citizens, the Rev. John Strachan, rector of St. James' Church (now Cathedral). When the invaders finally departed, they took with them the government mace, a treasured symbol of British sovereignty and authority that had been held in the highest esteem since the time of the province's birth in 1791. Its removal was a real slap in the face. For the next 121 years the mace was held by the Americans as a war trophy. Then, on July 4, 1934, as a result of a direct order given by President Franklin Roosevelt, the mace was finally returned to provincial authorities. Its arrival on board an American gunboat was one of the most spectacular events held during the city's centennial year. This mace is now on display at the Ontario Parliament Buildings.

July 2, 2000

Some Things Never Change

It often amazes me how two photos of the same part of Toronto taken almost a century apart can still look so similar in so many ways. Take the pair of photos that accompany this article, for instance. They were both taken from Queen Street near Grant looking west towards the very busy Broadview Avenue intersection. While the construction equipment, cars, and streetcar are obviously new, the streetscape itself hasn't changed all that much. Most of the old buildings still stand, though many have been altered, and not always in a sympathetic manner. The older photo is actually an image from a postcard manufactured around 1912 by the J. Valentine and Son Company of Dundee, Scotland, a fact borne out by the JV in the circle at the lower left. In the distance is a Toronto Railway Company wooden streetcar operating on the King route, which in those days ran along King and Queen streets from the Sunnyside loop west of Roncesvalles to Scarborough Beach Park, an amusement ground that occupied a large area on the south side of Queen Street between Leauty and Maclean avenues in the city's east end. The park was owned by the streetcar company and was a perfect way to utilize the company's streetcars in the evenings and on Saturdays, hauling people to and from the rides and events that took place throughout the spring, summer, and fall until the place closed down in 1925, just three short years after the Toronto Transportation

Both views look west from the corner of Queen and Grant streets to Broadview Avenue in the distance (c.1912 and 2000).

Commission took over the public transportation business. The TTC had no interest in running an amusement park. Moving people efficiently and quickly was a big enough chore. Soon after the park closed, land developers began buying up lots and building the houses that are now found on streets such as Scarborough Beach Boulevard, Wineva, and the south end of Hammersmith and Glen Manor. In late 1914, the eastern terminus of the King line was moved to Neville Park, where the 501 Queen cars loop today. In 1923, the King cars were rerouted up Broadview to a loop at Erindale Avenue, not far from where the streetcars connect with the Bloor-Danforth subway today.

As one can see on the modern view, the streetcar, in its modern form, is still part of the streetscape. Also visible in both views is the 1891 Broadview House Hotel (northwest corner of Queen and Broadview) and, to the extreme right, a former branch of the Canadian Bank of Commerce. This pillared structure was built in 1905–6.

July 16, 2000

Imposing Grid on Toronto the Good

When the original streets in the Town of York were laid out two centuries ago, virtually all ran east-west or north-south with little or no regard for the valleys and ridges, creeks and rivers that criss-crossed the topography. Because the pioneer land surveyors had no consistent point to start from, the shoreline being anything but a straight line, they created their own "base line," which was called Lot Street (referring to the hundred-acre pieces of property, or lots, that fronted on this thoroughfare). The name Lot was eventually changed to the present Queen, in honour of the young Queen Victoria. The surveyors sketched on their rudimentary maps things called concession roads, which over the years would evolve into the community's major east-west and north-south thoroughfares. The location of these concession roads was determined by the use of a Gunter's chain, a measuring device made of metal links that when stretched out measures sixty-six feet, or, in surveyor's terminology, a chain. These concession roads were laid out exactly 100 chains apart, and since 1 chain equals 66 feet, 100 chains equalled 6,600 feet, or a precise 1.25 miles. This then is why our major roads, both the east-west and the north-south variety, are exactly 1.25 miles apart. For instance, Bloor Street is 1.25 miles north of Queen, St. Clair 1.25 miles north of Bloor, etc., etc. In the same way, using Yonge Street as the starting

Looking east on St. Clair Avenue across Avenue Road, 1911 and 2000.

point, Bayview Avenue is 1.25 miles to the east and Bathurst 1.25 miles to the west.

In the photos accompanying this article, we can see what was originally known as simply the 3rd Concession Road. Of course, we don't call it the 3rd Concession Road any longer, but rather the more familiar St. Clair Avenue. While we can be precise on how the street got there in the first place, the origin of its name is less specific. One story has it named in honour of Augustine St. Clare, one of the characters in the book *Uncle Tom's Cabin*, which was published about the same time large numbers of people began taking up residence near the intersection of Yonge Street and the 3rd Concession in a community called Deer Park. If this is in fact true, somebody at some time got the spelling of St. Clair wrong.

July 23, 2000

The Latest in Hogtown Mascots

Several weeks ago I was the guest speaker at a major conference being held at the Harbour Castle Westin Hotel. While the subject of my talk was, of course, the history of our great city, the question that was on the lips of a large percentage of the 950 delegates at the luncheon was not "How do you pronounce Yonge, like sponge?" Nor was it "Just how safe are your streets at night?" Nope, the most frequent question was "What the heck's the story behind all the moose around town?" Well, after convincing them that a meal of moose hooves and bear navels really wasn't our national dish, I related the purpose behind Mayor Mel Lastman's multitude of moose and how later this fall the 326 mascots will be auctioned off, with the money raised going to various charities. As unimpressed with the promotion as many locals may be, I can tell you those moose are certainly a hit with the tourists. Even at the recent opening of the new 509 Harbourfront streetcar line extension along Queen's Quay (to Bathurst to the CNE Grounds) the appearance of the TTC's moose (did somebody call him Howard Moose-cow?) was one of the highlights of the day.

However, the concept of animals as city mascots is not new. Hogs have often found a place in descriptive comments about our city, and rightly so. At one time more hogs were processed in our city that in any other place on the continent save for Chicago. And remember when

Northwest corner of Front and Jarvis streets sometime in the late 1800s. Note the spire of St. James' Cathedral (left) and the domed cupola of the St. Lawrence Hall on both skylines.

Same view, 2000.

The TTC's Howard Moose-cow, one of 326 "moose-cots" roaming the city. Howard Moscoe is the Chairman of the Toronto Transit Commission.

Sesqui the Squirrel helped us celebrate Toronto's 150th birthday (the city's sesquicentennial) in 1984? Sesqui is still up a tree somewhere in High Park. And then there are cattle. In the old photo that accompanies this article we can see dozens of them on display at one of the city's busy downtown street corners. Since the photo was taken in the late nineteenth century, it's highly unlikely, even though His Worship has been around a long time, that he had anything to do with this particular promotion. Now, before anyone gets the idea that this herd consisted of stuffed bovine and was really some sort of pre-moose promotion, I'd better come clean. The intersection is, in fact, Jarvis and Front streets, and the building in the background is the old North St. Lawrence Market. In behind, the clock in the cupola identifies the gracious St. Lawrence Hall, and to the left of the view is the soaring spire of St. James' Cathedral. By the way, there is one similarity to today's moose promotion. These cattle were also to be auctioned off. However, that money went to the farmer. And the cattle? To the butcher.

July 30, 2000

Hope Floats in Captain John's Story

Toronto was a much different city back in 1970. New City Hall was still just that, new, having been open a mere five years. Toronto was between professional baseball teams, the Maple Leafs of the International League having passed on in 1967 and the Blue Jays still seven years in the future. The other Leafs, the hockey ones, with Ron Ellis as their top scorer, finished out of the playoffs that year. The 1970 skyline looked much different as well. There was no CN Tower, no First Canadian Place, and no Scotia Plaza. In 1970, the first building in the new T-D Centre complex reigned as the city's tallest, with the fast-rising Commerce Court about to appropriate that title. The city's waterfront was much different in the summer of 1970. There wasn't a hotel, restaurant, or condominium tower in sight. Nevertheless, something new was on the horizon. The slip at the foot of Yonge Street was about to get a "temporary" visitor in the form of a Manitoulin Island ferry boat. In fact, it was on August 8, 1970, exactly thirty years ago this coming Tuesday, that a young John Letnik rolled the red carpet down the gangplank and welcomed his first few customers aboard S.S. *Normac*. Captain John's Floating Restaurant was finally in business.

John Letnik was born in the Yugoslavian province of Slovenia at a time when few opportunities existed for its young people to, shall we say, better themselves. Even as a youngster John demonstrated that he had ambition. But it soon became obvious that if he was going to be a

MS *Jadran* in Adriatic service.

Captain John's MS *Jadran*, a true landmark on the city's ever-changing waterfront.

success he'd have to do it somewhere other than in his homeland. So at the age of just fifteen John packed up his meagre belongings and made for the Austrian border. His first attempt to escape failed. Nevertheless, his mind was made up. He'd try again. This time John was successful, and before long he found himself in Graz, Austria living in sparse accommodations with distant family members. John spent his days as a volunteer with the Red Cross helping others who, like himself, had fled their homeland eager to start a new life. One day a Red Cross official asked John if he'd like to go to Canada. The young man jumped at the chance. Sailing from Bremerhaven, John arrived in Quebec City on August 8, 1957. Interestingly, that day and month would be repeated several times as John's business career began to evolve. He'd been given a train ticket to Toronto and before long found himself standing, lonely and friendless, outside that city's somewhat forbidding Union Station. Now what? A young couple, sensing the seventeen-year-old was in a dilemma, approached him. The trio struck up a conversation, in German, the only language they all understood. Thanks to his new friends, John found not only a place to stay, but a job as a houseman at a golf club on the western outskirts of his newly adopted city as well. John remained at the golf course only a short time before a better paying position presented itself, this time as a dishwasher at the prestigious St. George's Golf and Country Club in Etobicoke. There he worked his way up to second chef, earning enough money to eventually buy his own restaurant, just a small place on Dundas Street near McCaul in downtown Toronto.

In 1966, John decided to take a well-deserved European vacation. It was while crossing the Atlantic on the S.S. *France*, where the meals were served in the ship's elegant dining room, that John came up with the idea of someday owning his own floating restaurant. That idea stuck, and on his return to Toronto, John began a search for the appropriate vessel. Three years passed before he found just what he was looking for, a badly weathered ex-Detroit fireboat, ex-tug, ex-Manitoulin Island ferry boat named *Normac*, well hidden away in the harbour at Wallaceburg, Ontario. On July 23, 1969, *Normac* sailed, under her own steam, for the Port of Toronto, where much work would be done to transform the sixty-six-year-old relic into Toronto's first floating restaurant. In the spring of 1970, *Normac* was relocated to her new, but "temporary" (at least according to Toronto Harbour Commission officials) berth at the foot of Yonge Street. On August 8 (there's that date again), "Captain" John served his first few customers. While he did, he couldn't help wonder whether his dream would be a success. John's plan was to move *Normac* to Ontario Place, a new waterfront attraction then under development south of the Canadian National Exhibition grounds. That didn't happen, and *Normac* remained at its "temporary" Yonge Street location for the next eleven years, until an incident with a Toronto Island ferry put the little vessel out of business. In the meantime, "Captain" John had started looking at ways to expand his popular waterfront restaurant and banqueting facilities. He set his sights on acquiring the sleek, 296-foot-long cruise ship MS *Jadran* (a word that means Adriatic in Yugoslavian) that had been built in 1957 in a shipyard on the Adriatic coast. It had five levels, 355 staterooms, and a maximum passenger capacity of over 700; over the years it had become a well-known visitor to numerous Black Sea ports as well as to Venice in Italy. Captain John arranged to purchase MS *Jadran* from the Yugoslavian government, and in the fall of 1975, assisted by a crew of sixteen, he sailed her across the Atlantic and through the St. Lawrence Seaway, arriving at her new home at the foot of Yonge Street on November 20, 1975. The conversion from cruise ship to floating restaurant quickly got underway, and in June of the following year MS *Jadran* was ready to welcome her first guests.

August 6, 2000

Brockville's Toronto Connections

While preparing my columns on Toronto's fascinating history, I often forget that other Ontario communities have interesting histories as well. That fact came through loud and clear several weekends back when I paid a visit to Brockville to attend a fundraising event at Fulford Place, a beautiful thirty-five-room, turn-of-the-century mansion overlooking the St. Lawrence River at the east end of that lovely city. Its owner and namesake, George Fulford, made his fortune marketing a cure-all product he called Dr. Williams Pink Pills for Pale People. With some of that fortune George built his riverside showplace, where he and succeeding generations of Fulfords entertained lavishly, many of their guests the nation's who's who. In 1991, the house, with its opulent French Rococo and Italian Renaissance furnishings, oriental ivory carvings, and European porcelain dinnerware nestled on three acres of landscaped property, was given to the people of Ontario by the Fulford estate. This provincial jewel is now held in trust by the Ontario Heritage Foundation (of which I'm proud to be a director) and lovingly looked after by the Friends of Fulford Place, a volunteer group of about seventy citizens who conduct tours of the mansion and raise funds for its ongoing upkeep. One source of funds is the guided "Ghost Walks" through Brockville's tree-lined side streets. The organization has just published a collection of these walks in book form. Details on purchas-

The former Johnstown District Court House and Gaol was designed by Torontonian John George Howard.

ing a copy, as well as when the house is open for tours, can be obtained by calling 613-498-3003 or emailing fulfordplace@recorder.ca.

Brockville was first settled in 1794 (one year after Simcoe selected Toronto as the site of a naval shipyard) by United Empire Loyalists led by William Buell. The community was first known as Elizabethtown (after one of King George III's daughter), a name changed to the present Brockville in honour of Sir Isaac Brock, hero of the War of 1812. As I went for a stroll through the downtown area, I may have been several hundred miles away from Toronto, but I suddenly spied a couple of Brockville landmarks that were intimately connected my hometown. At the apex of the Court House Square stands the former Johnstown District court house and gaol, an 1843 beauty designed by none other than Toronto's own "man for all seasons" John George Howard, who was also the architect of many of Toronto's early buildings and who, even while working on the Brockville project, was living in Colborne Lodge in High Park. The other streetscape feature that caught my eye was the wonderful City of Toronto coat of arms over the entrance to the downtown Brockville branch of the T-D Bank. The building was actually constructed in 1923 as that city's branch of the Bank of Toronto, which, in 1955, would join with another Toronto bank, the Dominion, to form the present T-D. When Toronto's coat of arms was sculpted on the facade of the bank in 1923, its appearance was

Toronto's coat of arms over the entrance to Brockville's T-D Bank.

not far off the original drawing, as history tells us, on a barroom floor in exchange for a few cool drinks. Perhaps because of the cleaner air in Brockville, that city's copy of our coat of arms is in remarkable condition. Of course, having been done before the original was "modernized," it is significantly different from those in use around our town — at least, in use until recently. That one too has vanished in favour of another version prepared for the new amalgamated City of Toronto in 1998.

By the way, if you like to bed and breakfast along the way, may I suggest the Gosford Place B & B (613-926-2164, gosfordplace@recorder.ca) a few miles north of Brockville. What this restored 1840 stone farmhouse may lack in riverfront views, it more than makes up for with incredible breakfasts, Mollie the puppy, and Charlie the kitten.

August 13, 2000

Good Lord!
It's Lieutenant-Governor Simcoe.

Well, they're still doin' it ... over and over and over again. They continue to call him Lord Simcoe. A couple of Mondays back, a lot of us celebrated Simcoe Day (while at the same time many others were honouring one of Honda's popular small cars). If I heard or read it once I heard or read it a dozen times. The day was set aside to honour Lord Simcoe. If I go to my grave having accomplished but one thing, please let it be the abolition of the term Lord Simcoe.

Let's go back to the beginning. This particular midsummer holiday was established back in 1869, right here in Toronto, by a few of our local politicians who believed that the hard-working citizens should have a midsummer break. Because it was meant to honour the citizens, the day was naturally given the rather bland title of Civic Holiday. A century later, Toronto city council, under then Mayor William Dennison, proclaimed that we do something very un-Canadian. We would rename the Civic Holiday and thereby honour someone who held a place of importance, not in someone else's history, but in our very own. And what better person to choose than John Graves Simcoe? Now, whether you find fault with either the man or his methods, it's a fact that Simcoe was our province's first lieutenant-governor and the man who recognized the significance of the site of the future city of Toronto by designating it, not as the site for the new capital of the young province (he had anoth-

Toronto's short-lived Lord Simcoe Hotel at the northeast corner of King and University in downtown Toronto. Opened 1957, demolished 1980.

er place in mind) but, because of its well-protected harbour, as the per-fect location for an important naval shipyard. It would be here, Simcoe proclaimed, that armed ships necessary for the protection of Upper Canada from American invaders would be constructed. Once the yard was up and running it wasn't long before a small community started to take shape nearby. It had streets and houses and a few rudimentary shops. Unimpressed with the name by which the area was known, Simcoe chose to call the town York to honour the Duke of York, King George III's second eldest son. No doubt Simcoe was trying to keep the monarch happy, for it was George who had much to say about the future of the colonies in British North America. Simcoe went about doing such things as were necessary to ensure that his new town, and his new province, would flourish. And flourish they have.

Now, here's my beef with the use of the term Lord Simcoe. It's plain, simple, and to the point: Simcoe may have been a lot of things, but there's one thing he wasn't. He was never a lord! Looking at his accomplish-ments not only in here in Canada, but on other world stages as well, it has been suggested that his elevation to the peerage was probably in the works. Perhaps it was his unexpected death in 1806 that precluded our

Governor (not Lord) Simcoe. Wonder if it's too late to bestow on him the title he deserves?

John Graves Simcoe becoming Lord Simcoe. And so, since that honour was never bestowed, the use of the term "Lord" is wrong. And while his wife, Elizabeth, may have been a lady, she obviously could not have been Lady Simcoe. What no doubt gave credence to the idea of Lord Simcoe was a hotel that opened its doors at the northeast corner of King Street and University Avenue in May 1957. It was called the Lord Simcoe, a name that concerned Ontario Premier Leslie Frost, who, after turning the traditional first sod on the building site, suggested strongly that the owners of the new hotel not invent history. It should be the Governor Simcoe, he exhorted. But there was a Governor Simcoe Hotel in Simcoe, Ontario and besides Toronto's had to at least be on a par with the Lord Elgin in Ottawa and the Lord Beaverbrook in Fredericton. So the Lord Simcoe it was. However, the new hotel was in business less than twenty-five years before down it came to be replaced by one of the Sun Life Centre's towers. I don't want to say that messing with history had anything to do with its demise, but...

August 20, 2000

$32-Million Facelift for Coliseum

They'll be raisin' the roof down at the good old "Ex" later this year. The roof they'll be raising is the one over the CNE's historic Coliseum. As well as raising the roof, there'll be a lot more going on as the old building is renovated, refurbished, and revitalized. The total cost of the new Coliseum Entertainment Centre will be a whopping $32 million, all of it privately financed. That's great, but what's it all for, you may well ask. Well, Toronto is about to get a second professional hockey team, to be known as the Toronto Roadrunners, whose home games will be played in the Coliseum's new-look Arena, which will have seating for more than ten thousand (with the top ticket selling for about twenty dollars) plus an additional thirty-seven luxury boxes which are now being offered for sale. Other traditional events will continue to be presented in the Arena, including the Royal's popular Horse Show as well as events related to the annual CNE.

Historically, our new hockey team began life as the Phoenix Roadrunners of the International Hockey League (IHL), an organization that got its start at the end of the Second World War. Its four teams, two in Windsor and two in Detroit, gave the area's returning hockey players a chance to pursue their love of the game. The IHL was successful from the start, and during the 1998–99 season more than 4 million fans cheered on their favourites in a league that has quadrupled

169

Work progresses on the new Coliseum at the CNE Grounds in the summer of 1921. It looks like the contractors won't meet that November 1921 deadline. They didn't.

An artist captures a Toronto Roadrunners game in the refurbished Arena sometime in October 2001.

since 1945 to sixteen teams. The origins of Toronto's new IHL team go back to 1996, when the Winnipeg Jets of the NHL moved to Phoenix, Arizona, became the Phoenix Coyotes, and started drawing fans away from the IHL's Phoenix Roadrunners games. It quickly became obvious that there just weren't enough fans to support teams in both leagues. As a result, the Roadrunners owners decided to relocate, with Toronto being their location of choice. This selection was made for a number of reasons, not the least of which was, in the words of Leafs captain Mats Sundin, "Toronto is the hockey capital of the world." The choice of the city's Coliseum as the Roadrunners' home arena is an interesting one, especially since at one time it was to be the home of another professional hockey team, the short-lived Toronto Toros of the World Hockey League. While no Toro games were ever played there, the Arena did have a sheet of ice installed for The Brier.

While on the subject of the Coliseum, its history is also of interest. It was constructed in 1921–22 to ensure that our city would be the permanent home of the newly established Royal Agricultural Winter Fair. The city was up against Hamilton, Ontario, a feisty community that also wanted the event. The promise to build a new million-dollar structure won the day, and construction of the new building was soon underway. The first edition of the Royal had been planned for late November of 1921, but unfortunately construction didn't keep pace with reality. As a result, the inaugural RAWF didn't take place until the following year. The Royal's new home was trumpeted far and wide as the largest building under one roof in the world. In 1997 the Coliseum became an integral part of the mammoth National Trade Centre, to which it is connected through the dignified Heritage Court. It is anticipated that the Toronto Roadrunners hockey team will play its first game in the Arena at the Coliseum Entertainment Centre in October 2001.

August 27, 2000

* The project was held up for a variety of reasons. As a result it is now anticipated that the new hockey team will play its first game in the renovated Ricoh Coliseum on November 1, 2003. The delay has resulted in the cost of the project escalating to $38 million.

Mackenzie Was Railway King

I've been following with great interest the various news stories concerning the impact privatization is having on the operations of some of the large municipal transportation companies around the world. The most recent was a less-than-positive story on the London underground system (the Tube) and how it has suffered since some components of this once-proud system have been privatized. Here in Toronto, public transit has been a municipally controlled entity since an act passed by the provincial government on June 4, 1920, allowed for the creation of the Toronto Transportation Commission, which went into business for the first time on September 1, 1921. The name was altered to Toronto Transit Commission with the imminent opening of the first section of the Yonge subway line, the 12-station, 4.8-mile stretch between Union Station and Eglinton Avenue. Prior to its conversion to municipal control, the service was provided by a succession of private companies; the first, The Toronto Street Railway (and its successor the Toronto Street Railway Company) ran a horse-car service from 1861 until 1891. When the franchise expired, the city dabbled with the idea of assuming operations. However, the costs associated with acquiring new equipment and making the necessary repairs to a system that had been allowed to deteriorate badly, plus the immense financial outlay necessary to upgrade the system to electric operation, forced the city fathers to hand the operation over,

Born near Kirkfield, Ontario in 1849, Mackenzie died in his Toronto residence "Benvenuto" on the Avenue Road hill in 1923.

once again, to the public sector, this time in the form of the Toronto Railway Company (TRC). Municipal control would have to wait. While the introduction of transfers (prior to the TRC era additional fares were required whenever a passenger changed streetcars) and the electrification of the system were well received by the public (incidentally, both features were demanded by the city as part of the new agreement of 1891), the overall performance of the new company did much to hinder, not help, the growth of the city. In fact, try as the city officials might to get the TRC to expand its service into the outlying areas and to add additional equipment to lessen the crowding at rush hours, their attempts were constantly rebuffed. Track and right-of-way maintenance was another problem. It too was costly and did little to improve the company's return on investment. All in all, it was not a happy situation for the streetcar patron. Unfortunately for the city, when the matter was presented to the highest courts in England, the judge confirmed that the TRC was bound only by the city boundaries in place at the start of the company's monopoly, that is 1891. Even though the city had expanded tremendously since then, public transportation need not (and, as a result of the court ruling, would not) keep pace.

The aggravation that resulted from the company's ongoing concern for profit before service led to the eventual ousting of the private company in favour of municipal control and the birth of our TTC. I often wonder whether the lessons learned from the events that transpired during the years that the system was operated by private, profit-driven concerns will be remembered when the subject of privatization appears on the Commission's agenda.

Sir William's likeness is but one of the carvings in the Sculpture Garden that was created when a windstorm felled many of the lofty trees around the Sir William Mackenzie Inn in Kirkfield in 1995. The Inn was originally Sir William Mackenzie's summer home.

One of Sir William's Toronto Railway Company early electric streetcars testing its new cowcatcher safety device, c.1893.

While on the subject of the Toronto Railway Company, the man who was at the helm for most of its existence is about to be honoured with a Historic Sites and Monuments Board of Canada historic plaque, thereby confirming Sir William Mackenzie's important role the early development of our country. As difficult as Mackenzie must have been to work with, history now recognizes him as one of the country's most successful entrepreneurs. Like many of the other giants of his day, people such as Sir Henry Pellatt (Casa Loma), Frederick Nichols (Canadian General Electric), Hart Massey, and Timothy Eaton, Mackenzie was often ruthless and unforgiving in his business technique. History now tells us that such traits were often necessary to mould a young, uncertain country into an independent and respected nation. To paraphrase the wording on the new plaque, Mackenzie, along with his partner Sir Donald Mann (whose residence out the Kingston Road gave us the street name Fallingbrook), built the Canadian Northern Railway, thereby opening large areas of the West to settlement. By 1915, it had evolved into a transcontinental railway, only to suffer financial setbacks as a result of the outbreak of war; it eventually became part of the Canadian National railway system. Mackenzie diversified his interests, entering the lucrative fields of mining and shipping, and helped develop Ontario's first major hydro-electric power system, ensuring his electric streetcars in Toronto would have a supply of relatively inexpensive power generated from the falling waters at Niagara. He also controlled transit systems in Winnipeg, Great Britain, and South America. Today's Brascan began its existence as one of Mackenzie's many entrepreneurial creations.

September 3, 2000

Toronto Water an Old Problem

I can't recall a summer when the city's numerous waterfront swimming beaches have been closed so often. The prime reason for these closures is something that happened in our city's past. It's a somewhat delicate subject and something most people don't like to talk about these days. I was first introduced to the situation when I worked for the old Ontario Water Resources Commission, the forerunner of today's Ministry of the Environment. Throughout the later part of the nineteenth century, and well into the twentieth, the City of Toronto annexed a large number of surrounding communities. This was because places such as Yorkville, Parkdale, Riverdale, West Toronto Junction, and North Toronto were financially unable to provide their citizens with such necessary amenities as public transportation, garbage disposal, a reliable supply of clean drinking water, and subsequent disposal of the waste water. Since they were unable to tax at the same rate as the city, the money just wasn't available to address these problems. As a result, many of the smaller communities were forced to ask the big city to annex them. The problems then became Toronto's problems. With the ever-increasing pressure on the city budget, one relatively inexpensive way to get rid of waste water was to build what were termed combined sewers. In this type of sewer, the contaminated water was conveyed in a sort of trough affair enclosed within the main storm sewer. During periods of dry weather the

Pollution didn't seem to bother these bathers down at Sunnyside Beach in 1934. Perhaps the nearby "tank" was full. The schooner in the background was to be intentionally burned, the flames hopefully attracting customers to the park.

contaminated water was segregated from what little storm water there might have been in the sewer. The contaminated flow was eventually redirected to a sewage plant where limited treatment was afforded prior to its discharge into the lake or bay. However, during a heavy downpour the relatively clean storm water would fill the sewer and mix with the contaminated wastes, resulting in the entire contents being discharged into the bay or lake through the numerous storm outfalls situated all across the city's waterfront. Obviously, the more frequent the rainfalls, the more polluted the waterfront became. Over the years, extensive and expensive rebuilding of the ancient sewer systems lessened the contamination problem, but didn't end it.

Now, years later, the city is still working on the problem. The latest technique (first suggested in the 1920s) is the construction of a series of huge holding tanks along the waterfront. They are designed to hold all contaminated water, storm and sanitary, which previously entered the lake. These holding tanks will allow the waste water to be redirected for treatment during periods of low flow. This program is not yet in place, and the beach closures continue. Whether this multi-million-dollar project works and the pollution of Toronto's waterfront will be a subject only read about in history books published in the future remains to be seen.

The popular High Park Mineral Baths in the twenties.

Earlier this century, Torontonians came up with their own way to combat contamination of their city's swimming beaches. Up on Bloor Street West, near Clendenen Avenue and opposite High Park, Dr. William McCormick, a well-known physician and pioneer in the use of Vitamin B for the treatment of multiple sclerosis and Vitamin C to fight infectious diseases, opened a pair of mineral baths, the first in 1913, the second three years later.

The "Minnies," as they became known, served the nearby community (as well as bathers from distant corners of the city) until the TTC's right-of-way for the Bloor-Danforth subway forced their closure in the early 1960s. Nearby, the beautiful building that housed the doctor's Strathcona Hospital still surveys the scene from the hill north of Bloor Street. (I'd love to hear from readers with any stories about Dr. McCormick.)

Down on the western waterfront, the Toronto Harbour Commission was faced with two problems that were keeping crowds away from its Sunnyside Amusement Park. The first was the extremely cold waters of Lake Ontario that resulted from colder than normal summers in the two years that followed the park's opening in 1922. The second was the inevitable contamination from nearby storm outfalls. Officials were able to get around these troubles by constructing what, at the time, was the

Although it was officially know as the Sunnyside Outdoor Natatorium, everybody knew the place as "the tank." This photo was taken in the fall of 1932.

largest outdoor heated swimming pool in the world. Measuring 350 feet by 75 feet with a maximum depth of 9 feet, "the tank" (as all the locals referred to it, and as most still do) could accommodate 2,000 bathers. Admission was thirty-five cents for adults and a dime for kids. Construction costs approached $75,000, far too much to simply call it a swimming pool. The Harbour Commission christened it the Sunnyside Outdoor Natatorium. Today, it's the Sunnyside-Gus Ryder Pool.

September 10, 2000

Not All in Favour of City Hall

You know time is slipping away when events you think happened just a short time ago actually took place many years ago. For instance, while most of us still refer to our municipal building on Queen Street West as New City Hall (and it even looks like a new city hall), the truth of the matter is that the structure was thirty-five years old last Wednesday. By Toronto standards that makes the building almost ancient. Nowadays, most people, citizens and visitors alike, regard the building, in its magnificent setting within Nathan Phillips Square, as one of the city's premiere architectural highlights. It's interesting to note, however, that not everyone was happy with its selection. Many of the comments made soon after the announcement, on February 28, 1958, that forty-eight-year-old Finnish architect Viljo Revell's design had been chosen over 419 other submissions were less than gracious.

Take for instance the criticism of world-renowned architect Frank Lloyd Wright, who not only suggested that the city's plans for a civic square would result in "a tombstone which will mark where the city fell," but went on to describe the new City Hall design as the work of an architect who was simply eager "to win his spurs." He suggested that no self-respecting architect would have even thought of entering the city-sponsored design competition. Local architect Charles Dolphin was upset with the judges' decision for a different reason. He believed

180

Crowds contemplate a model of Toronto's new City Hall in a downtown store show window. The facial expressions run the gamut from WOW! to WHAT?

that with the country's billion-dollar deficit there was no reason to send a million dollars of taxpayers' money to Finland, the million dollars being the amount owed Revell based on 6 percent of the building's estimated construction cost of $18 million. By the way, in true Toronto tradition, that million-dollar figure would nearly double before the new City Hall's doors finally opened seven years later. I describe it as a Toronto tradition because the approved estimate for a building that would become today's Old City Hall (which is, thankfully, still standing just across the street from the new and obviously the reason why the present Hall is described as New) was initially pegged at $250,000. By the time its doors opened 101 years ago tomorrow that figure had risen to $2 million.

Other caustic comments about Revell's creation included those of former city mayor Leslie Saunders, who remarked, "That funny-looking thing? It's too modernistic and futuristic to suit me." Alderman (later Mayor) Phil Givens said it would have been his third choice. But, he went on, "What can we do. We're stuck with it." Many others were disappointed that the team of five internationally respected judges hadn't selected a design submitted by a Canadian. The closest a Canadian came to winning was when Torontonian David Horne was

Toronto's New City Hall appears in this 1972 postcard put out by the Holiday Inn, which had recently opened next door. At that time, the Holiday Inn Downtown-Toronto (as it was then called) was described as the largest in the chain. It later became the Colony Hotel, and in early 2003 it was purchased by the University of Toronto to be converted for use as a new student residence.

chosen as one of the eight finalists. He was among five from the States and one each from Denmark and Finland. Horne's only comment following the judges' decision was that he was happy to receive his $7,500 prize and was glad the competition was over. Offsetting these negative comments were the expressions of support from the ordinary public. The *Toronto Telegram* summed it up with the banner headline "IT'S A BEAUTY." So it was and so it remains.

By the way, another local event that was sharing newspaper headlines with the selection of the design for Toronto's new City Hall was the installation of Toronto's new pedestrian crosswalks. Like Revell's design, those crosswalks also came in for a lot of negative comments.

September 17, 2000

Man Behind Mineral Baths

A couple of weeks ago I wrote about the Mineral Baths (or "Minnies" as many knew them) that were located on the north side of Bloor Street, opposite the west end of High Park. The baths were built and operated by Dr. William J. McCormick, a Belleville-born physician who practised at Chicago's Northwest Hospital before moving to west Toronto. In 1906 he established a nerve sanitarium in a beautiful big house on Gothic Avenue (which is still visible from Bloor Street) that was later to be known as the Strathcona Hospital. The mineral baths were constructed originally for the use of his patients, but they were eventually opened to the public. Interestingly, from the start the baths were open to both sexes, a first in the history of the province. The "Minnies" were closed to permit construction of the new Bloor-Danforth subway, which opened in 1966.

The doctor was well-known in professional circles through his studies of vitamins C and B-1. McCormick believed that polio, MS, sleeping sickness, and amnesia could be conquered through the use of high doses of the latter while the former could cure gall stones, TB, and blood poisoning. McCormick and the Nobel Prize-winning chemist Linus Pauling were good friends, both sharing similar beliefs on the value of high doses of Vitamin C. One of McCormick's most intriguing, and controversial, experiments had to do with the development of a device that allowed

Dr. William McCormick and his "fireless pipe," 1936.

The good doctor's High Park Mineral baths, c. 1920.

Dr. McCormick's Strathcona Hospital is seen to the extreme left of this c.1918 photograph from the City of Toronto Archives. In the middle of the view are the good doctor's High Park Mineral Baths. To the extreme right is an unpaved Bloor Street with one of the Toronto Civic Railways' streetcars on the Bloor West route. Originally this part of Bloor Street was virtually impassable due to the presence of a deep gully. In this view work is progressing on filling this barrier using hundreds of tons of dirt and rubble. Today, the Bloor-Danforth subway runs under this part of the street.

cigarette smokers "to gain the effects of nicotine without inhaling the noxious fumes and carbon monoxide associated with burning tobacco."

McCormick died in 1968 (cause unknown) at the age of 88 and is buried in Park Lawn Cemetery.

September 24, 2000

Watch Out for Streetcars

Recently, city police officers, along with staff of the TTC, conducted a week long "Streetcar Watch Program" during which special emphasis was placed on the increasing incidence of car and truck drivers passing the open doors of streetcars stopped to take on or discharge passengers. With nearly 150,000 people using streetcars daily on the city's various streetcar routes, the problem has become increasingly serious. In fact, since 1995 a total of eighty-three people have been hit while entering or exiting streetcars. Obviously, that's eighty-three people too many. And how many near misses is anybody's guess.

Incidentally, passing those open doors is not only a selfish act on the part of inattentive motorists, it's also in contravention of Section 166 of the Ontario Highway Traffic Act, which states that drivers must stop two metres behind the streetcar's open doors. Subsequent conviction can result in a fine of $110 and the loss of three demerit points. Worse, however, is the possibility of serious injury or death. And it's not as if that regulation is a new one. A check of the records indicates that it wasn't long after the first electric streetcars began roaming Toronto streets in the 1890s that a law was enacted to charge drivers of horse-drawn wagons, and even bicyclists, who passed streetcars discharging passengers. With the arrival of the automobile early in the twentieth century, the law was rewritten to include the "horseless carriage," with one of the earliest con-

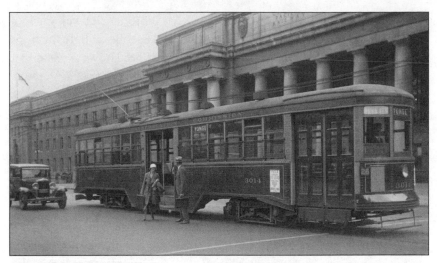

Both these motorists demonstrate the correct way to approach a stopped streetcar with doors open. Above a Peter Witt streetcar lets passengers off in front of Toronto's new Union Station on Front Street. Below, a passenger boards one of the recently introduced PCC cars on the St. Clair route, 1938.

victims of a pioneer Toronto motorist occurring in 1917. By the way, cyclists continue to be the main culprits in passing open streetcar doors. Many claim they didn't know they too had to stop. Well, they do.

Even though the two photos that accompany this column are nearly seventy years old, they nevertheless show the proper way to treat a stopped streetcar. In one, snapped in 1932, a motorist sits well back of a Peter Witt streetcar on the Yonge route as passengers alight in front of Union Station. The other view, taken in 1938, shows a passenger boarding one of the TTC's sparkling new President's Conference Committee (PCC) Streamliners that had only recently entered service on the St. Clair line. The motorist, patiently obeying the law, waits for the motorman to close the doors.

While on the subject of streetcars in general, and the St. Clair route in particular, there's an interesting struggle going on at City Council with the future of the TTC's now abandoned car house and storage yard on Wychwood Avenue, just south and west of the St. Clair/Bathurst intersection. It was here that hundreds of streetcars (including PCC 4031 seen in the photo) were stored and serviced. The conundrum facing council is that some members want to simply sell the property to a developer who will then demolish the buildings, build houses, and probably walk away with a tidy profit. Councillor Joe Mihevc and other members, reacting to the wishes of most of the people who live in the area, would prefer to turn most of the property into parkland. The only building that would be retained is the centre portion of the carhouse itself, which could subsequently be used for a variety of community purposes. Interestingly, this old structure has been part of the community almost as long as there has been a community in this part of the city. Built in 1913, it was used to house nine of the large, green streetcars operated by the Toronto Civic Railway. The TCR had been established by the city in 1911 to provide transportation to and from the terminals of the city lines out into the fast-growing areas around the city, areas that the owners of the city system refused to serve, arguing there was no profit for their shareholders in such superfluous operations. The Civic Railway officials opened the St. Clair route, Yonge Street to Caledonia Road, in the summer of 1913. It was the second of their "suburban" lines, the first being Gerrard in 1912. These two routes were followed by Danforth (in the fall of 1913), Bloor West (1915), and Lansdowne (1917).

October 1, 2000

Unearthing Necropolis's Past

This year marks the 150th anniversary of one of the city's most interesting cemeteries. The Toronto Necropolis, which is located just north of Riverdale Farm and overlooks the Don River, Bayview Extension, and Don Valley Parkway, was established in 1850 by a group of city businessmen. Though hard to believe in this day and age, the cemetery's fifteen-acre site, which was described in ancient guide books as bordered by Sumach Street, Castle Frank Road, the Plank Road (now Winchester Street), and the beautiful (!) Don River, was selected because of its "serenity and attractive outlook."

Necropolis was initially run as a business until it was purchased by Toronto Trust Cemeteries in 1855. The Trust had been established years earlier to provide a final resting place for the indigent and those whose religious beliefs (or lack thereof) prevented them from being buried in the few churchyards that existed in the young city. When the Trust's old cemetery at the northwest corner of a remote Yonge and Bloor streets was ordered closed by the province, the organization (which still operates under the title Mount Pleasant Group of Cemeteries) purchased the Necropolis and turned it into a non-profit, non-sectarian burial ground. It was to the Necropolis that the unclaimed remains from Yonge and Bloor cemetery were reinterred in an area now known as the "Resting Place of the Pioneers." Over the intervening years the Necropolis became

Small's Grand Opera House on Adelaide Street West. Some said Small met his end in the theatre's ancient furnace.

"home" to some of the city's most illustrious citizens. Among them are Toronto's first mayor, William Lyon Mackenzie; world champion sculler Ned Hanlan (whose father is recognized in the title of Toronto Island's Hanlan's Point); Anderson Ruffin Abbott, the first Canadian-born black physician (and a good friend of president Abraham Lincoln); Joseph Bloore (Bloor

Ambrose Small, where are you?

John Doughty; some thought he knew what happened to "Ambie." If he did, he never spilled the beans.

Street — the final "e" disappeared somewhere along the way); and *Globe* newspaper founder and "Father of Confederation" George Brown. Oh, and John Doughty is there too.

While most members of this group enjoy some level of recognition, I wonder how many recognize the last name in the list? Probably very few until I associate him with his boss, Toronto theatre owner Ambrose Small. Small disappeared from the face of the earth in early December 1919, mere hours after selling his various theatrical holdings, including the popular Grand Opera House on Adelaide Street just west of Yonge, for $2 million. Less than a month later John Doughty, who had been Small's personal secretary for more than seventeen years, also went missing. At first, many thought the quiet, retiring Doughty had something to do with Small's disappearance, or perhaps even with Small's murder, a possibility that was becoming more and more likely. The police, however, were pretty sure Doughty had taken advantage of the situation and had simply chosen that time to run off with $105,000 worth of bonds owned by Small.

Arrested in an Oregon lumber camp a year later, Doughty was returned to Toronto, where he was found guilty of robbery and sentenced to six years in the Kingston pen. He was never charged with the kidnapping of his boss. Four years and nine months later, Doughty was released and immediately went into seclusion. If Doughty had any answers as to the ultimate fate of Ambrose Small, a case that has still to be solved, he took it to his grave in the Necropolis.

October 8, 2000

Hurricane Hazel Brought
Tragedy to Toronto

On this day forty-six years ago, reports issued by the local weather office predicted that the rain, which had been falling on and off in the Toronto area for the past few days, would continue overnight. The rain would change over to occasional showers the following day. For most people the weather for Friday, October 15, 1954, though not pleasant, was certainly nothing to worry about. Sure, if you had read the paper closely, or listened attentively to the in-depth weather reports on radio or the city's only television station, CBLT channel 9 (a position on the dial — remember dials? — that the station retained until 1956), there were the remnants of a hurricane called Hazel somewhere south of the border. But who ever heard of a hurricane making its way into Ontario? That was a weather phenomenon most believed was reserved for the citizens of the southeastern United States.

However, as Friday wore on, the impossible became fact when the storm reached Lake Ontario, regained its intensity, and took dead aim on the unsuspecting City of Toronto and its environs. Worst hit was the west end, with suburban communities such as Woodbridge and Port Credit suffering major storm damage and loss of life. To the north the fertile Holland Landing became a huge lake, while the Don and Rouge rivers to the south and east experienced greatly increased volumes of water, with some resulting damage. The worst, however, had

Firemen recover the body of one of their fallen comrades, one of the many victims of Hurricane Hazel.

been reserved for many neighbourhoods adjacent to the Humber River, with the Town of Weston suffering the most. In fact, it was here that a quiet community street called Raymore Drive was obliterated by the raging river. Almost all of its houses were swept into the torrent, including the one shared by the Edwards and Neil families, who lived in number 148. A granite memorial in Mount Pleasant Cemetery coldly reminds us of the three adults and six children who lost their lives that tragic evening. In total, thirty-six people living in houses on the ill-fated Raymore Drive became Hazel's victims.

A little further south the Humber claimed more lives when its powerful debris-filled waters swept a fire truck and its five-man crew into oblivion. Deputy Chief Clarence Collins and firemen Frank Mercer, Roy Oliver, David Palmateer, and Angus Small, all members of the Kingsway-Lambton volunteer fire brigade, had responded to a call to assist a stranded motorist. A memorial plaque affixed to a boulder in a park adjacent to the now-calm Humber River records their deed. Early in November, the men were eulogized at a special service

A flag-draped fire truck, preceded by a Toronto Fire Department vehicle, makes its way to the cemetery following a memorial service for the five lost Kingsway-Lambton firemen.

at Kingsway-Lambton United Church, which was attended by fourteen hundred mourners and six hundred firemen who represented forty fire departments throughout the province.

October 15, 2000

History Is All in the Cards

One of the great pleasures in my life (in addition to being married to a fine woman and having a classic old car — and if she's reading this, in that very order) is visiting a sale that features old postcards. And what's even better is finding, among the thousands offered for sale, a real gem. That's exactly what happened one rainy day last spring. When we arrived, the Humber College gym was filled with dealers and eager deltiologists (that's the twenty-dollar-word for postcard collectors). Not taking time to even hang up my coat, I was on the hunt. To say there were lots of postcards is a major understatement. There were thousands, including cards featuring the faces of well-known people of days gone by, views of the Caucasian and Rocky Mountains, old steam trains, old autos, old people, flags of the world (many of which no longer fly), and on and on. That's great, but where are those old Toronto cards? Let me check over on that table. Here's one I want, and another, and another. All three pretty nice finds, but the best was yet to make its appearance. Way over in the corner was a table with a two-buck-a-card box full of old Toronto views. Squirrelled in amongst them was an absolutely exquisite card that featured a painting of the old Toronto waterfront. The reverse side told me that the sender, identified only as H.T.H., was "having a nice trip" and wanted the recipient, one Harry G. Hall (brother?) of Mill Hall, Clinton

Toronto skyline from the ferry boat wharf near the foot of Bay Street. This view, which appears on the cover of my new book, *Toronto Sketches 6,* was originally reproduced on a postcard dated 1909.

While it's hard to pinpoint exactly where the artist stood while painting the older view, this view from Lakeshore Boulevard West between Bay and Yonge streets is my best guess.

County, Pennsylvania to know it. The cancellation of the one-cent King Edward VII (of King Edward Hotel fame, or is it the other way 'round?) stamp confirmed that the card cleared the Toronto post office at 2:00 PM, August 28, 1909, a Saturday (!!) afternoon.

But this wasn't just a postcard — at least, not the type that most people are familiar with. In fact, it was a painting reproduced in postcard format by Raphael Tuck & Sons, an English company that began as picture framers in 1866 and five years later designed its first Christmas cards. In 1894, the company entered the picture postcard business. The card I purchased was listed as number 2594 in its "Oilette" series, "Oilettes" being described as "The Aristocrats of Picture Postcards." While the work is unsigned, some Tuck expert might be able to identify the artist by his (or her) style. The card is of special interest to me because of its precise content. Visible (left to right) are the A.R. Williams Machinery Company building on old Lake Street, (about where the Toronto Harbour Commission Building stands today), the clock tower of City Hall at the top of Bay Street, and, at almost dead centre, the fifteen-storey Traders' Bank Building that has stood at the northeast corner of Yonge and Colborne streets since 1906. When it appeared in this painting it was the tallest building, not just in Toronto, but also in the entire British Empire. To the far right is the instantly recognizable spire of St. James' Cathedral, an element of the city's skyline since the tower's completion in 1874. The small Toronto Island ferry on the west side of the Bay Street wharf is (possibly) the *John Hanlan* (burned at Sunnyside as an attraction in 1929) while on the east side of the same wharf is either the ferry *Primrose* or *Mayflower* (the two were almost identical). The two lake boats in the Yonge Street slip, one a two-stacker, the other with a single stack, are difficult to identify. Perhaps a reader knows their names.

So pleased was I to obtain this unique postcard, I've featured it on the cover of my new book *Toronto Sketches 6* (Dundurn Press, $17.99), a collection of almost one hundred "The Way We Were" columns that have appeared in the *Sunday Sun* over the past couple of years. The book is available at better bookstores or through the Sun News Research Centre (416-947-2258) or on the web at www.canoe.ca.

October 22, 2000

Some Issues Never Go Away

One way to come up with ideas for this column is to simply read the newspapers. Not today's newspapers, mind you, but the papers of yesteryear. Scattered throughout those ancient issues are reports that describe people, places, and events that have become ingredients in Toronto's evolution from what was basically a small, rather nondescript community to the great city we all enjoy and respect today. During these forays into the past, I frequently come across headlines that, except for the date at the top of the page, could be describing events that are taking place right now. Here are a few of the more interesting reports (with some paraphrasing) complete with the date the stories first appeared.

WHERE TO PUT TORONTO'S GARBAGE POSES A MAJOR PROBLEM

A serious problem is fast developing in the disposal of refuse according to city hall officials. In a few months Toronto will have no place to dump its refuse with the size and urgency of the problem evidenced by the fact that the department now disposes of 1,000 truckloads a day. Of particular concern is incombustible waste as dis-

In the summer of 1954, trucks drop their loads of garbage along the east bank of the Humber River, just north of The Queensway. The railway and traffic bridges over the Humber and the Palace Pier dance hall can be seen in the distance.

tinct from household garbage the disposal of which will be adequately provided for with the opening of the new Commissioners Street incinerator. At present the city is dumping at a temporary site in Long Branch, an arrangement that is subject to 1-day notice. "There is no place left in the city", advises a city official. "Every piece of land that once might have been suitable has been developed. And the city is hemmed in by municipalities each jealously guarding its own dumping sites."

For twenty-five years dumping went on in the Greenwood Avenue area, until 1952, when a 30-acre gravel pit, 125 feet deep, was totally filled. Dumping then shifted to marshland south of Eastern Avenue and east of Leslie Street. This location too is nearly filled. A few weeks later a city newspaper carried details of a secret report suggesting dumping industrial wastes in a variety of locations around the city, including

Waste materials from a variety of construction projects around the city were trucked to the waterfront (here in front of the Toronto Harbour Commission Building), where they were used as landfill.

along the fertile marshes in the Eglinton Avenue flats (adjacent to the present Jane and Eglinton intersection), the pit of the Toronto Brick Co. (now the brick works site in the Don Valley north of the Bloor Street viaduct), Woodbine park between O'Connor and Dawes Road, and in the gullies of the Scarborough Bluffs. That article concluded with the following: "The main method of disposing of Toronto area industrial wastes at present is either to truck to areas beyond the metropolitan boundary or dispose of it out in Lake Ontario."

And when did those articles appear? The first was on May 5 and the second on June 25 in the year ...1954!!

CITY LOSES OLYMPIC BID

It was learned late yesterday that the Olympic Games will not be held in Toronto. However, the city will try to persuade the International Olympic Committee that the next Olympic Games scheduled for 4 years from now should be held here.

The games in question were those for the year 1960. The news report, published on April 15, 1955, went on to blame the failure of the city to be awarded the Games on the fact that it had failed to complete the official Olympic Committee application that had been forwarded to the city in October 1954. No one at City Hall could account for the missing application form. Nevertheless, some city officials were confident that another try for the 1964 Games would be successful since we already had several of the necessary venues: Maple Leaf Gardens, the CNE Grandstand, and for yachting, canoeing, and rowing, the waters of Lake Ontario. Miffed that the city failed to get the 1960 games because it didn't advance its case before the Olympic Committee, the ubiquitous Allan Lamport once again piped up, "If you don't promote, you don't get." Oh, Rome got the Games in 1960, Tokyo in 1964.

METRO EXPRESSWAY NETWORK TERMED VITAL TO DEFENSE

Today, many believe that the sooner we get rid of the Gardiner Expressway the better. Multi-lane at-grade thoroughfares or an "expressway in a tunnel" are usually offered as solutions. Interestingly, when officials began bandying about something they simply called a cross-waterfront highway back in late 1947 (a road that was expected to cost $3 million, a figure that by 1962 had jumped to $95 million), the driving public just couldn't wait for work to begin. And to get the work started on this important thoroughfare as soon as possible Alderman (later Mayor) Allan Lamport suggested making it a toll road with the fees helping to pay for its swift construction. Imagine, a toll road in Ontario. Never! By the way, as much as this new highway was needed to move Toronto's ever-increasing number of cars, trucks, and buses, it, and others, would be absolutely necessary to ensure that the city could be evacuated when radar warnings from stations in the Arctic confirmed an imminent attack by Russian warplanes. Or so visiting U.S. Civil Defense Administrator Val Peterson warned local civil defense authorities, including General Frank Worthington, Peter's father. And the year of this declaration? 1955.

October 29, 2000

Public Transit a "Private" Matter

One of the questions put to the voters on Election Day 1920 (back then municipal elections were always held on New Year's Day regardless of snowstorms and hangovers) was whether they wanted to change the way the city's streetcar system was being operated. Up until then public transit had been in the hands of a succession of private entrepreneurs, starting in 1859 with a service from Yorkville to the St. Lawrence Market provided by the stagecoaches of part-time funeral director Henry Burt Williams. Then came the horse-drawn streetcars of the privately owned Toronto Street Railway Company, followed in 1891 (after a short but unsuccessful try at municipal operation) by the electric cars of the Toronto Railway Company. This latter company was under the absolute control of one of the nation's most successful and hard-nosed businessmen, Sir William Mackenzie.

Initially, these companies provided a satisfactory service, but with the arrival of Mackenzie's company in 1891 the service began to deteriorate. The main reason for this deterioration was the need for Mackenzie to ensure that his stockholders realized a profit on their investments. So instead of spending money to buy more streetcars to improve service in town or investing thousands of dollars in new track and overhead to service the sparsely inhabited outlying suburbs, Mackenzie pinched his pennies. In his mind, spending huge sums of

"Large" Witt 2392 makes its way through the busy Dundas Street/University Avenue intersection in 1941.

money to purchase more streetcars to lessen rush hour crowding or to modernize an aging fleet was simply out of the question. As for servicing the suburbs, that too was just a waste of money. His reaction to spending any money on upgrading the system could doubtlessly be accounted for by the fact that the company's monopoly would expire on August 31, 1921. As the years went by, city officials constantly fought with Mackenzie in an effort to gain improved transportation services for the citizens. Mackenzie was just as eager to make as much money as possible in the time left, both for his shareholders and for himself.

With the arrival of Election Day 1920, the answer to the question of how to handle the city's public transit problems was a foregone conclusion. That day an exasperated electorate voiced its collective opinion and overwhelmingly recommended that public transportation become a municipal responsibility. With their vote, the citizens had set the wheels in motion to create what we know today as the Toronto Transit Commission. The next step in the evolution of the TTC took place on June 4, 1920, when the provincial government authorized the

Another Witt northbound on Bay Street pauses at the Queen Street corner to let participants in one of the city's numerous War Bond Parades pass by, c.1944.

Council of the City of Toronto to establish the Toronto Transportation Commission (the word "Transportation" became "Transit" coincident with the opening of the city's first subway in 1954). The new Commission's prime responsibility would be the consideration of "all matters relating to local transportation in the city." There were many additional clauses in the Act, one of which defined who could and could not be appointed a commissioner of the new TTC. Initially, politicians were ineligible, in an effort to ensure there would be no political interference. Today, all seven TTC Commissioners are elected city politicians. The first TTC commissioners were three prominent city businessmen: jeweller P. West Ellis, hotel proprietor George Wright, and building contractor Fred Miller. The trio was appointed on August 5, 1920, with the Commission's first General Manager, H.H. Harvey, coming on board less than two months later. The most important part of the takeover was the proclamation that the new TTC's mandate would come into effect at midnight (Standard Time) Thursday, September 1, 1921.

One of the first steps the TTC took to ensure rapid improvement in streetcar service was the purchase of the most technologically advanced equipment (we'd call it "state of the art") then available. In April 1921, an order was placed with a Montreal-based Canadian Car and Foundry for one hundred "Peter Witt motors" and sixty "Witt trailers." An additional forty "motors" were ordered later that same year. This revolutionary type of streetcar had been developed under the guidance of Peter Witt, a transit expert who had done much to improve the street railway system in Cleveland, Ohio. In fact, every time the TTC purchased one of the Witt vehicles (in total the Commission bought 350 "motors" and 225 "trailers") Peter Witt and his associates received a fifty-dollar royalty. The first Witt cars entered service on October 2, 1921, and were soon found carrying ever-increasing numbers of passengers on routes all over the city. Torontonians finally had a transit service of which they could be proud. Of the multitude of Peter Witt streetcars that did such yeoman (or is it yeocar) service in the TTC's pioneer years only one remains, #2766. This car was one of one hundred similar vehicles that, being almost five inches shorter in overall length than the original Peter Witts, were described as "small" Witts. Retired from service years ago, this historic vehicle now languishes on the lower level of a former TTC bus garage. At a recent TTC meeting, Commissioner (and St. Paul's West Ward 23 candidate in the upcoming municipal election) Joe Mihevc moved that staff undertake to return the car to operational status. Wouldn't it be fitting to have old 2766 front and centre when the Commission celebrates its eightieth anniversary on September 1, 2001?

November 5, 2000

Man Who Would Be Mayor — Wasn't

As I'm sure you are all aware, tomorrow is Municipal Election Day here in Ontario; while we've all heard a great deal more about the Federal election, in my opinion, at least, those who are chosen to run things locally are equally, if not more important than the politicians sent off to that never-never land up in Ottawa. I mean when was the last time a federal MP fixed a pothole on your street, kept public transit a viable alternative to the automobile, or paid real attention to the plight of the homeless? There are some exceptions, but for the most part what affects us the most is looked after right here at City Hall. So get out and mark your ballot. If you don't and we get a bunch of duds you've no one to blame but yourself.

Speaking of marking your ballot, we've come a long way from that day in late March 1834 when our city's very first municipal election was held. Earlier that month the Town of York had been elevated to the status of city so that taxes could legally be collected on real property. The money so collected would be used build such civic amenities as sidewalks and sewers. "Plus ça change ..." With the creation of the new City of Toronto (the bill that created the city had also restored the community's original name), it became obvious that an election would have to be conducted to see who would run the place. For administrative purposes the new city (population 9,254) was divided into 5 wards (named after a quintet of saints, namely Andrew, David, George, Lawrence, and Patrick), with 2 aldermen and 2 councilmen to be elected in each ward. At that time the voters didn't select the mayor. That wouldn't happen until 1858. Toronto's first mayor would be appointed by the council as a whole. More about that later. As Toronto was a child of the province (which it remains, for better or for worse), it was the provincial bureaucrats who would decide the city's future. One of their first decisions was that the city's first civic election would be held on Thursday, March 27, 1834.

In 1834, there were several differences between the way Torontonians of the day and those of November 13, 2000, would select the local representatives. The most obvious were that only males would vote, and the vote would not be cast by the secret ballot method we cherish today. Rather, the eligible voter simply walked into his designated tavern-turned-polling-booth-for-the-day and shouted out his choice for all to hear. Another major difference was the use of the candidate's political party affiliation as the reason for voting him (again, males only) in or out. Such affiliations tend to be downplayed today by most, but certainly not all, candidates. Nevertheless, back in 1834 that party connection was pretty much the only reason for selecting an aspirant to the City Hall, such as it was (the run-down former Town Hall at the southwest corner of King and Jarvis, which for the event had been altered in name only). Interestingly enough, the party that gained the upper hand in the city's

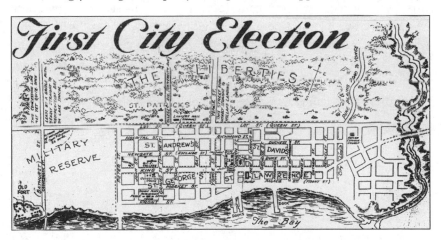

The new City of Toronto as it looked on the eve of the first municipal elections, March 27, 1834.

Dr. John Rolph, the man who would be mayor, and wasn't.

first elected council was made up of "Reformers." Their only goal that first election seemed to be the defeat of the "Tories," a group made up of members and friends of members of the so-called Family Compact, who lived by the credo "what's good for me is good for you." The anti-establishment feeling reigned that Election Day, and by the time the dust had settled the Reformers had elected a total of ten members, two more than the Tories could muster. As for the position of mayor, that would be left up to the will of the new council. At first it appeared as if Dr. John Rolph, the recently elected reform aldermanic candidate for St. Patrick's Ward, who had the respect of many of the Tories, would get the nod. But when the most zealous of the Reformers learned that Rolph had the support of the Tories, they decided to support someone who was a true Reformer (i.e. hated by the opposition). When Rolph learned of this he resigned from council, leaving his nemesis William Lyon Mackenzie, the reform alderman from St. David's, a clear shot at the Mayor's chair. And so it was that the man who would be mayor, wasn't. The next best choice was. Mackenzie held that exalted position for less than ten months, replaced by Toronto's second mayor (you never hear about those who came second) lawyer Robert Baldwin Sullivan.

November 12, 2000

Motoring Back to Yesteryear

Ah, the smell of a new car. Or in the case of the Filey family, new cars. Yup, both my wife and I have brand new vehicles, Yarmila her distinctive PT Cruiser (for which she had to wait almost six months) and me with a new Saturn coupe. Oh, before I take flack for adding to the earth's environmental concerns, this pair of four-cylinder vehicles replaces a pair of less fuel efficient, more environmentally unfriendly vehicles that we've had for years. So there. As I went to pick up my new car from Ted over at Downtown Saturn I got to thinking, as I am wont to do, what it must have been like when the first cars began to appear on Toronto city streets. I wondered if there were environmentalists who were glad to see those awful polluting horses being taken off the city streets. Would those pioneer "horseless carriage" salesmen dicker with the price? Did "horseless carriages" have a new "horseless carriage" smell? And just who was the first person to operate a "horseless carriage" in Toronto?

While I can't answer the first two questions with any authority, a story in the June 25, 1923 *Evening Telegram* newspaper revealed that Toronto's first "motor owner" was Dr. Perry Doolittle, a medical practitioner who lived at 619 Sherbourne Street. In fact, Doolittle held claim to being not only the city's first "motor owner" but its first used car owner as well, his "motor" having been purchased second-hand

Torontonians have always been fascinated with "motors," as witness this crowd gathered opposite the Automobile & Supply Company store on King Street East, c.1903.

from Colonel T. Moodie of Hamilton in 1898. The Colonel was famous in his own right, holding the title of Canada's first automobile owner. He was also one of the first to dicker with the car's price by convincing the customs people that the American-built Winton import should be classed as a locomotive (with an import duty of 25 percent) and not a carriage (import duty 30 percent).

Now, before I run afoul of the car experts out there, the statement I have made regarding first "motor owner" refers to first owner of a gasoline-powered vehicle. To be historically accurate, there were a number of other "horseless carriage" experiments going on at about the same time the good doctor was puttering around town and even earlier. They included a variety of battery-powered vehicles, with the one built by William Still in his Yonge Street factory for patent attorney Fred Fetherstonhaugh being one of the earliest. Fetherstonhaugh recharged his car's battery by "borrowing" electricity from the wires of the radial streetcar that operated along Lake Shore Road in front of his "Lynne Lodge" residence in suburban Mimico. In fact, for a time these

His new "motor" and his best girl in High Park. c.1904.

so-called "electrics" seemed to be the way of the future. Parkers Cleaners on the east side of Yonge Street north of Bloor had an electric delivery truck, while downtown the big Robert Simpson store had several. The post office had a few little ones scooting around town picking up and dropping off sacks of mail. Timothy Eaton's larger-than-life son John Craig Eaton was another pioneer "motor owner," though he was a believer in the gasoline versions, having a Winton "1-lunger." John C. also arranged to have the family company sell the Chalmers and Waverley motors via their popular catalogues. And if you think that the roads and streets around town are crowded with cars today, that situation is not new. In fact, participants in the prestigious Glidden Tour were discouraged from driving through Toronto because of the large number of cars on the city streets.

November 19, 2000

This Plant Generated Some Steam

At the far east end of Toronto Harbour, squeezed between the Ship Turning Basin and Unwin Avenue (a street named after pioneer Canadian land surveyor and Toronto civic government official Charles Unwin), stands the hulking R.L. Hearn Generating Station, a mammoth facility that when put into operation nearly a half-century ago was the largest steam generating plant in the entire country. Today it sits quietly, out of commission and awaiting a future that, to say the least, is uncertain. Work on the Hearn began in 1949, at a time when the province was desperately in need of additional electrical generating capacity. The recent world war had curtailed the building of new plants to such an extent that when peace returned in 1945 there just wasn't enough electricity to supply the needs of the hundreds of new factories that had opened to supply the needs of a war-starved populace. Frequently, this lack of power led to severe restrictions on its use and subsequent "brown-outs" during which street and house lighting in areas of the province (including Toronto) would fade to an eerie glow. The first unit of the new $67-million R.L. Hearn Generating Station went on-line in late October of 1951, generating 88,000 kilowatts of electricity. Initial plans called for the Hearn to produce 536,000 kilowatts, though with upgrades over the ensuing years this figure ultimately reached 1,200 megawatts before the plant was finally taken off-

Aerial view of the R.L. Hearn Generating Station on Toronto's eastern water-front. Note the original stacks and the new, taller ones after plant expansion in the early 1960s.

line in 1983. Some of the plant's generators and transformers are still used to stabilize imbalances in the city's electrical grid system.

In the Hearn's early years its original four generating units were powered by steam that came from the burning of huge quantities of coal, some 800,000 tons of which were stored on property to the east (and visible at the top left of the accompanying aerial photo). Forty tons of coal were consumed per unit per hour, with 155 million gallons of lake water converted to steam each day. Much of the steam was condensed back to water and reused in the boiler. For many years, a cooling water discharge from the Hearn made for great fishing at the little wooden one-lane bridge on Unwin Avenue. While attempts were constantly being made to keep particulate stack emissions to a minimum, it was eventually decided to convert most of the plant to natural gas. In the 1970s, 85 percent of the electricity was produced using this method. In addition, to reduce stack gases even further a monstrous seven-hundred-foot chimney was built to disperse emissions over as wide an area as possible.

As for the name of the plant, Richard Lankaster Hearn was one of the Hydro Electric Power Commission of Ontario's (later simply

Richard Lankaster Hearn (1890–1987).

Ontario Hydro and now Ontario Power Generation) first employees, joining the seven-year-old company in 1913. In later years the Toronto-born U of T graduate strongly advocated the generation of electricity through the use of nuclear fuels, and he was somewhat surprised when it was announced that the nation's largest coal-fired plant, a process about which he claimed to know nothing, was to be named in his honour. Hearn served as chairman of Ontario Hydro in 1955–56, being appointed following the untimely death of the previous chairman, Robert Saunders, in a plane crash. R.L. Hearn died in 1987 at the age of ninety-seven.

December 3, 2000

* Plans are underway to convert the abandoned hydro plant into a mammoth motion picture studio.

The mothballed Hearn and its seven-hundred-foot chimney today.

Toronto Then and Now

For those of us who were born and grew up in this great city, it's difficult to convey to newcomers just how much Toronto has changed in a relatively short period of time. As a member of the "1941 club," I've seen remarkable changes that have transformed the city from a place where going out for a nice Sunday night dinner usually meant visiting the grandparents or heading downtown to one of the city's large hotels (the Royal York, King Eddy, and The Embers dinning room at the Prince George come to mind). I also remember the Town Tavern on Queen Street near Yonge and their wonderful beef torpedoes. Sunday sports, newspapers, and movies were out of the question when I was a kid. Going to morning service at Eglinton United followed by Sunday School under the tutelage of Grant Shaver were the highlights of my Sabbath.

I remember the excitement of riding the country's first subway in March of 1954, and the Saturday afternoon in 1958 when the steel skeleton of the new Union Carbide Building on Eglinton Avenue East collapsed. Traffic was so light that even though some girders fell out onto the street only a couple of parked cars were struck. Such an occurrence today would create a catastrophe. I remember when an order of fish and chips was thirty-five cents (if you got halibut, the good stuff), when peddling drugs simply meant delivering prescriptions for a drug

Some of the most remarkable changes in the look of Toronto have taken place along the waterfront, where we're told more changes are about to happen. These two photos from my book *Toronto Then & Now* were taken from approximately the same vantage point. Note the proud Toronto Harbour Commission Building right on the water's edge in the top photograph. Today, though still standing, this same building is landlocked.

store (as I did), and when my dad had to fill out forms to purchase a case of beer at the government "drug store," places that always seemed to be lit by twenty-five-watt bulbs. I remember Power stores, Bargain Benny's (an "Honest Ed" wannabe), Danforth Radio, Eaton's Annex with its wooden escalators and an ice cream waffle shop in the tunnel that connected with the main store on Queen. And I remember wizened old men driving horse-drawn carts that patrolled the city's back alleyways.

My public and high school principal and teachers never had first names (nor did they ever work to rule), the ink wells were filled by some teacher's pet, and once a year we'd have Cadet Inspection Day. I remember when the fare for a ride on one of the Island ferries was a pair of streetcar tickets (one to go over, the other to come back), when there was a huge White Rose gasoline sign on the Terminal Warehouse Building, and when the tallest building on the city skyline was the Bank of Commerce (which is still there as Commerce Court North though virtually undetectable in amongst all the other modern skyscrapers.)

December 10, 2000

Island Airport Bridge Up in the Air

Guess what? I finally found something that's been going on longer than the U.S. presidential race (which, by the time this column appears, may have been settled, but somehow I doubt that). Our debacle revolves around whether or not to build a bridge across the West Gap to serve the airport at the west end of the Island. Many believe this connection will greatly improve the viability of Toronto City Centre Airport, a name chosen a few years ago to replace the term Toronto Island Airport and to emphasize the proximity of the airfield to downtown Toronto. For the record it should be stated that the airfield has actually had three names; the first was Port George VI Island Airport, a mouthful of words selected by city council to honour King George VI's first visit to Toronto in 1939, the year the first few aircraft began using the new Island facility. The monarch was accompanied by Queen Elizabeth, now the Queen Mother.

When the first of the Island airport drawings appeared in 1935, one of its major features was to be, not a bridge, but rather a tunnel running south from the foot of Bathurst Street under the West Gap to a large parking lot adjacent to the runways. Work actually began on this tunnel well in advance of any construction on the airport itself. The purpose of the tunnel was twofold, first as an access to the future airfield and second, and perhaps more importantly at the time, as a way of putting men

This is but one of the many, many plans submitted over the years for Toronto Island. This one, dated 1952, features that elusive tunnel under the four-hundred-foot-wide West Gap along with other Island "amenities."

who were still suffering from the effects of the Great Depression back to work. In April 1935, the federal government of R.B. Bennett set aside $1 million for the project, and within six months work on the city-side approach had been started, steel piling installed, and dredging completed for the necessary coffer dam across the channel that would permit tunnelling to begin. It was all in vain, however, for 1935 happened to be a federal election year. When Bennett's government was defeated by that of William Lyon Mackenzie King one of the first things the new premier did was to rescind all funding for the tunnel. No money, no tunnel.

Work did get underway on the airport, however, and by 1939 it was fully operational. But the idea of that fixed link never really went away. Every few years new plans for the future of the Island were released and almost every time a link was included, though now instead of an expensive tunnel officials were promoting a less expensive bridge. That's not to say the tunnel concept was totally dead. In fact, as recently as 1979 a private Montreal aviation company proposed building a $5-million pedestrian tunnel so Montreal and Ottawa-bound com-

At first access to the airport was by this unnamed rope ferry fashioned out of a converted scow. Though classed as temporary, it lasted twenty-five years until the present *Maple City* was acquired in 1964. A back-up boat, *Windmill Point,* arrived in 1985. The original airport terminal is in the distance.

muters could "walk" to the airport. Seven years later the new City Express airline predicted that by 1988 a vehicle tunnel costing between $12 million and $18 million would be in place. Needless to say, nothing happened. Then, in 1996, the fixed-link proponents switched from the idea of a tunnel connection to a bridge connection, not unlike the streetcar bridge over the old West Gap first proposed in the late nineteenth century. It would have permitted Toronto's less affluent citizen a "one-seat, one-fare" ride to the Island playground.

Even more recently — earlier this year in fact — city council finally approved a bridge connection, provided a few minor details were ironed out before work could actually begin. One of the details was just who would pay for the multi-million-dollar structure. This, plus a few other imponderables, eventually led council to ask that another "Future of the Island Airport" study be undertaken, this time to determine whether the airport has a future in the "new" Toronto. And if it has, would a bridge connection be necessary to ensure that future? Here we go again. I daresay our American neighbours will have their president before we have our Island bridge. On the other hand, if the report states that the airport has no future a second vote will be requested and another report will be sought ... manual recount!!

December 17, 2000

Memories of Christmases Past

Not long after the Toronto Transportation Commission went into business on September 1, 1921, (it was renamed the Toronto Transit Commission coincident with the opening of the Yonge subway nearly thirty-three years later) the new organization published the first edition of its new in-house magazine called *The Coupler*, an interesting title that referred to the apparatus that joined two streetcars together to form what was called a train. Many readers will recall the Witt trains that operated for years up and down Yonge Street and, in more recent times, the PCC train that ran back and forth along Bloor Street and the Danforth between Jane loop in the west and Luttrell loop in the east. *The Coupler* was filled with folksy stories about TTC staff, new appointments throughout the Commission, health advice, retirements, and interesting features on what was new and what was old throughout the Commission. All these years later, *The Coupler* is still being published and continues to be eagerly anticipated by staff and retirees alike.

In my collection I have two rather special editions of the magazine, each with cover artwork that is evocative of the era in which it was published as well as of this wonderful time of the year. The first, from 1936, shows passengers rushing to board an eastbound Peter Witt streetcar (vehicles that were introduced to Torontonians about fifteen years earlier) at the Yonge Street stop. In the top background are the

Artist Jimmy Frise's view of Christmas in Toronto, 1936.

huge crowds that peered into the famous Christmas windows at the old Eaton store on the north side of Queen. And at the lower left, check out Santa with his collection pot and the corner newspaper boy. And there in the bottom right, helping pedestrians and vehicles through the busy intersection, is a Toronto traffic officer resplendent in his warm fur hat. I wonder how long the streetcar operator retained that happy face? In the second view, it's 1942 and Canada is at war. Nevertheless, Torontonians try to enjoy Christmas, though sadness had invaded many city homes. In this sketch, one of the TTC's modern PCC cars, again eastbound on Queen, loads and unloads at a downtown stop. Santa is still ringing his bell while a trio of young ladies ogle an RCAF officer, and some poor old guy's bike has just gotten a flat tire.

The artist of both views was the remarkably talented Jimmy Frise (1890–1948), who was best known throughout Canada and the United States for his column titled "Birdseye Centre" (later renamed "Juniper

And again in 1942. Both sketches from the TTC's in-house *Coupler* magazine.

Junction"). Jimmy was born on a farm on Scugog Island and educated at local schools (he has been recognized by the installation of an Ontario Heritage Foundation commemorative plaque nearby). The young man was a naturally gifted and self-taught artist who got his start here in Toronto. For many years his work appeared in the *Toronto Star* and *Star Weekly* and later nationally in the *Weekend Magazine*. It was in this publication that Frise and newspaperman/humorist Greg Clark joined forces, creating features that were read and enjoyed by thousands.

Merry Christmas and Happy Holidays everyone!!

December 24, 2000

Old City Hall Bells Still Toll for Us

There are lots of sounds that can be defined as true "sounds of Toronto." Take, for instance, the sound of streetcars crossing the "diamonds" at a busy downtown intersection. Or the whistle of a departing Toronto Island ferry boat, the rousing chant "Go Leafs Go" at the Air Canada Centre, or the cuckooing and chirping of those traffic lights that help assist the visually impaired at several crowded street corners. Then there's the sound of the bells in the tower of Old City Hall. On four different occasions each hour — the quarters, the half, and the full hour — the mighty trio of bells shout out the time, their thunderous sound cascading down Bay Street, up into Chinatown, west through the tranquil grounds of Osgoode Hall, and east to the raucous corner of Yonge and Queen. The sound of the City Hall bells has been heard by citizens and visitors alike for exactly one full century, for it was precisely one hundred years ago this evening, December 31, 1900, that the bells rang out for the first time.

While a clock and set of bells for the tower were always in architect Edward James Lennox's plans for the city's new Municipal Building, one city alderman, John Hallam (of Hallam Avenue fame), had an idea that went one step further. While the building was taking shape, he asked that city council look at the possibility of including in the tower "a chime of musical bells." Hallam's idea was to have the chimes play two

City officials inspect the trio of bells prior to their placement in the clock tower. Terauley (now Bay Street) is in the background. Note the name of Old City Hall's architect, Edward James Lennox, written on one of the bells.

or three times a day, with a different song for each day of the month. He even had some ideas as to what those tunes should be. He selected some well-known hits of the day, such as *Rule Britannia*, *The Maple Leaf Forever*, and *Men of Harlech*, as well as tunes we seem to have forgotten, such as *All Among the Barley*, *The Sicilian Mariners Hymn*, and *Canada, Our Home* to name a few. While the cornerstone of the building was

City Hall, Toronto, Canada

Postcard view of Toronto City Hall. The absence of the Cenotaph in front of the building dates the view pre-1925, the year the war memorial was dedicated.

tapped into place on November 21, 1891, it took almost eight more years before the city council was able to move in. Throughout this period of time it seems that somebody forgot to order the tower clock and bells. It wasn't until July 7, 1899, or less than three months before the Hall's official opening, that the order was placed with the manufacturer, Gillett and Johnston of Croydon, England. What the architect requisitioned (as described on the invoice, a copy of which was given to me by the company during a visit to the foundry several years ago) was a "#5 Ting Tang" clock with twenty-foot dials, at a cost of $12,500, "fixing and every expense included." The bells were to be three in number; the largest, to strike on the hour, was to be cast with the dimensions five feet, ten inches high and six feet, ten inches wide. It would weigh exactly 12,768 lbs. The middle bell was to be three feet, seven inches high and four feet, four inches wide. It would weigh 3,382 lbs. The third, and smallest, would be three feet high and three feet, six inches wide. It would weigh 1,993 lbs.

The total cost of the trio of bells, this time including the cost of "hoisting" along with "fixing and every expense" was five thousand dollars. This price included inscribing the names of the architect, the mayor, the City Hall committee members, and the aldermen on the outside surface of the large bell. For some reason, city council had budgeted only $5,000 for the project, which, with freight and duty charges added, came to a grand total of $19,750. To get around the problem, staff was simply ordered to find the rest of the money "somewhere," and they did. Soon after the clock mechanism and bells arrived, they were hoisted up the outside of the three-hundred-foot tower using a small steam engine and steel wire ropes. The hoisting of the large hour bell took place on November 26, 1900, and, as can be expected, drew a huge crowd of spectators. It was decided to hold off ringing the bells until midnight, December 31. That way they would ring in not only the new year of 1901, but the new century, the twentieth, as well.

And so it was that exactly one hundred years ago tonight that Torontonians heard the sound of Old City Hall's friendly and reassuring bells for the first time.

December 31, 2000

*While on the subject of birthdays, December 31 also marks the fortieth anniversary of CFTO-TV, Channel 9 (later Cable 8). The station went on the air for the first time at precisely 9:45 on New Year's Eve, 1960. The first program was a special telethon broadcast from brand new studios erected on a $132,000, 30-acre parcel of land out in the wilds of suburban Agincourt. The telethon raised more than $200,000 for developmentally challenged children. One of the hosts that evening was the well-known Joel Aldred who, along with John Bassett, Ted Rogers, and Foster Hewitt, was the prime mover in the establishment of the nation's first privately owned television station.